lak works

KB051975

1

Park
Campus
Waterfront

landscape architecture korea

『laK WORKS』 시리즈는 한국 최초의 조경 전문 잡지인 월간 『환경과조경』에 게재된 작품을 선별해 한 권의 책으로 묶는 기획입니다. 『laK WORKS 1』은 2014년 1월호부터 2016년 12월호까지 소개한 국내외 조경가의 작품 중 의미 있는 이슈를 생산할 수 있는 23개 작품을 선정해 수록했습니다.

laK WORKS is a publication project that selects and combines the works from landscape architecture korea, a monthly landscape architecture magazine which is the first of its kind in the country, into a series of volumes.
laK WORKS 1 is a collection of the 23 landscape architecture works carefully chosen from the magazines published from January 2014 to December 2016, which we believe will contribute to bringing up productive discussions and raising valuable questions.

laK WORKS 1

Publisher Park Myung Kweon 박명권
Editor laK (Monthly Magazine) Editorial Team 환경과조경 편집부
Editorial Design Cho Jin Sook 조진숙

Address (06674) 2F, Seocho-daero 62, Seocho-gu, Seoul, Korea
　　　　　　 서울시 서초구 서초대로 62 (방배동 944-4) 2층 (우06674)
Tel 82-2-521-4626 **Fax** 82-2-521-4627
E-mail klam@chol.com **Homepage** www.lak.co.kr

Published by Jokyung Publishing Co. 도서출판 조경
First Published March 12. 2018
Fixed Price USD 80 (80,000원)

Printed in Korea

Contents

Part 1. PARK

Part 2. CAMPUS

Part 3. WATERFRONT

Part 1.

PARK

Garden of Migration

Agence APS

Landscape Architects Agnece APS
Engineering Sitétudes
Lighting Agence Lumière Régis Clouzet
Mediterranean Vegetation Consultant
Olivier Filippi
Agronomist Véronique Mure
Collaborator Biotope, Enviroconsult,
Antoine Bruguerolle
Client Ministère de la Culture et de la
Communication
Location Marseille, France
Area 15,000m² (Fort), 6,500m² (Planting)
Cost 6 millions euros
Completion 2013
Photographs Agence APS, Agence Lumière

Along the costal area of Marseille, a massive inner-city reconstruction project is on the way. Between the city and the ocean, at pier J4, the Museum of the Civilizations of Europe and the Mediterranean(MuCEM) revealed its unmissable horizontal presence. The focal point of the project is located along the high wall of the old fortress; it required a receptive attitude to bring out the program from the very site. This sensual and dialectic garden contains both natural and human history and is itself "a open collection." The design of unstructural shape of the garden signifies the wealth of time itself. The walk through the garden reinacts history like a travel diary on the day and with each name.

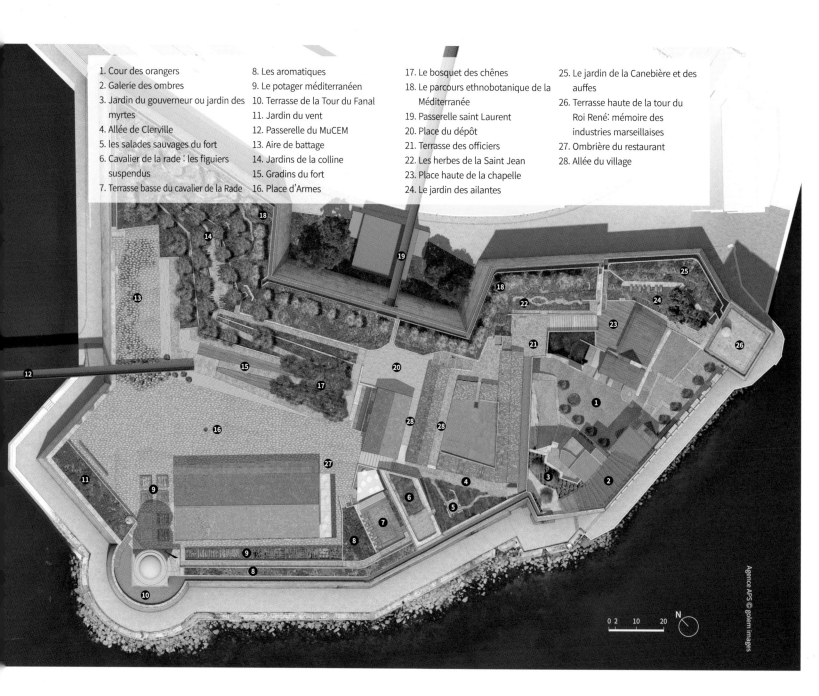

1. Cour des orangers
2. Galerie des ombres
3. Jardin du gouverneur ou jardin des myrtes
4. Allée de Clerville
5. les salades sauvages du fort
6. Cavalier de la rade : les figuiers suspendus
7. Terrasse basse du cavalier de la Rade
8. Les aromatiques
9. Le potager méditerranéen
10. Terrasse de la Tour du Fanal
11. Jardin du vent
12. Passerelle du MuCEM
13. Aire de battage
14. Jardins de la colline
15. Gradins du fort
16. Place d'Armes
17. Le bosquet des chênes
18. Le parcours ethnobotanique de la Méditerranée
19. Passerelle saint Laurent
20. Place du dépôt
21. Terrasse des officiers
22. Les herbes de la Saint Jean
23. Place haute de la chapelle
24. Le jardin des ailantes
25. Le jardin de la Canebière et des auffes
26. Terrasse haute de la tour du Roi René : mémoire des industries marseillaises
27. Ombrière du restaurant
28. Allée du village

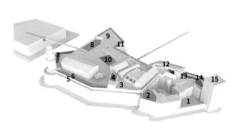

Composition of Garden of Migrations

Building ■
Open Space ■
Garden ■

Fortress buildings and spaces

©Agence APS

The Garden of migrations rising up at the port of Marseille reminds us of the interchange of cultures across the Mediterranean Sea and the exchange of plants through them.

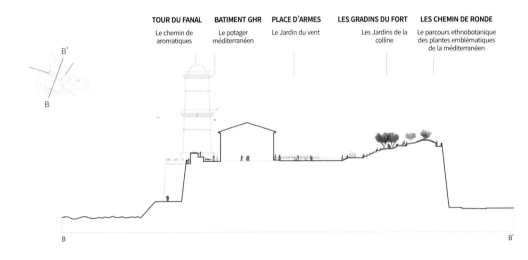

TOUR DU FANAL	BATIMENT GHR	PLACE D'ARMES	LES GRADINS DU FORT	LES CHEMIN DE RONDE
Le chemin de aromatiques	Le potager méditerranéen	Le Jardin du vent	Les Jardins de la colline	Le parcours ethnobotanique des plantes emblèmatiques de la méditerranéen

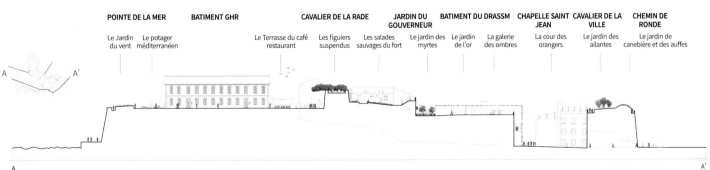

POINTE DE LA MER	BATIMENT GHR	CAVALIER DE LA RADE	JARDIN DU GOUVERNEUR	BATIMENT DU DRASSM	CHAPELLE SAINT JEAN	CAVALIER DE LA VILLE	CHEMIN DE RONDE
Le Jardin du vent / Le potager méditerranéen		Le Terrasse du café restaurant / Les figuiers suspendus / Les salades sauvages du fort	Le jardin des myrtes / Le jardin de l'or	La galerie des ombres	La cour des orangers	Le jardin des ailantes	Le jardin de canebière et des auffes

Garden of Migration in the port of Marseille with its influx of people and flora reminds of the exchange of culture and of flora that came with it in the Mediterranean region. Consecutive 15 pieces of works(gardens) reject ornamentality of the usual garden but bring forth sensual experience to the visitors with their variety of leaves and textures and the scents of the flora. Multi-layed entrance and floors insures the visitors of interesting elements regardless of time of a year, be it spring or winter, regardless of visitors attentive or distracted. Especially, the dry garden adds values to the Mediterranean flora.

In the backdrop of the blue sea of the port city of Marseille, the old fortress is connected to the bridge as a new museum.

15 Gardens-Trails

Garden-Trail consists of 15 consecutive pictures.

1. La cour des orangers: It reminds us of the Mediterranean, the first court of Almohad Caliphate's Garden, or Courts of Orangers in Grand Mosque in Cordoba or Sevilla.

2. Le jardin des myrtes: It is full of delicate scents of flowers and leaves, and its name associates us with *Myrtus communis* in Alhambra Granada. Myrtus and pomegranate forms the rectangular aisles. Its formal grandiose design reminds us of the dignity of Viceroy of the past.

3. Les salades sauvages du fort: This is a place of tribute to the plants of reconquest that overcame adverse environment. This is a garden for those plants that reconquested on the barren soils on their own.

4. Les figuiers suspendus: Figs are the symbolic trees of Mediterranean. It is natural that figs have a place here. Perpetual fruiting of figs symbolizes prosperity in the various cultures in the Mediterranean.

5. Le chemin des aromatiques: Mediterranean Cuisine can not be without aromatic plants. So they take their place next to the vegetable garden(Le potager mediterranean). Aromatic plants of grown just upto hands' height argue for touch. There are time, sage, sariette, marjoram, lavandula, and hyssup.

5-1. Les odeurs de la garrigue: Some of bush plants in the barren land have great scents(about 10% of them). This scent defines the Mediterranean air. These definitely have a place here.

Le chemin des aromatiques and Le portager méditerranéen

6. Le potager méditerranéen: It is Mediterranean vegetable garden of winter and summer, of native vegetables or the foreign ones that now have their places in "traditional" cuisines like ratatouille or bohemian.

7. Le jardin du vent: It is a garden of graminae. The graceful swing of these plants reminds us of wind and gives a chances to talk about their strategy to spread their seeds.

8. L'ire de battage: Open to Northwest and thus to mistral, L'ire de battage reflects on La Crau or Larzac Plateau where the wind and sheep form the dynamic of the scenery.

9. Les jardins de la colline: A thornbush is a symbol of flora in the hills of Marseille, and most of all it also represents the great Mediterranean tradition of agriculture, forestry and ranching. The mosaic scenery has been sculpted by fire for 5,000 years from human activities.

10. Le bosquet des ches verts: Mediterranean landscape cannot be described without the forests. Most of the forests are filled with holm oaks, which fueled most of the domestic cooking ovens. The need for such use perpetuated the widespread of the coppice trees. What would be the future of forests in Mediterranean region?

Terrace of Les figuiers suspendus

The bridge between MuCEM and Saint-Jean Fortress and the Gradins du fort. At this stage, it leads to the Les jardins de la colline, which shows the traditions of Mediterranean agriculture, forestry and animal husbandry.

11. Le parcours ethnobotanique des plantes emblatiques de la mediterranean: The immense anthropogenic botanical history in the Mediterranean is the pinacle among the trails: the intersection of Islam and the Judeo-Christian cultural traditions on plant uses. The long flower garden is the fresco of the immense history told by those plants.

12. Les herbes de la St. Jean: "Healing herbs" in the herb garden of Saint John were picked on June 24th when John the Baptist was born. The name of the fortress was after the Saint.

13. Le jardin des ailantes: The tall *Ailanthus altissima* warns us on the potential problems of introducing foreign species from other countries.

14. Le jardin de la canebière et des auffes: this garden trails toward the city area and cannabis. This garden tells us the importance of ropes and esparto products in Mediterranean ports like Marseille, which is made from cannabis and from auffres(fibrous plants in Provence).

15. Le jardin des industries marseillaises: the high terraces of the King Rene's inner court completes the trails, and the memories on plants, Marseille and the industries in the Mediterranean all come alive. In the future, the commercial history of spices, coffee, oil, soup, anise spice, cotton, dye will be staged at the center of the garden.

L'ire de battage

Garden into the future

Garden of Migration leads us to contemplate on permeability, flow, immigration and evolution that lie beneath the conflict for survival between native plants and foreign ones. The ecological wealth, plants and activities around them in Modern Europe and the Mediterranean aid us with unstructured memories of knowledge, know-how, know-act, and know-be that prove our shared history.

The immigration in the past asks us about the immigration of the future. Population movement today is much faster and more frequent than in the past, and such anthropogenic activities are carved on the environment. How would global warming affect plant immigration? What would the natural environment look like in the future? How would our cultural surrounding integrate the coming of new species that is often described as invasion? These questions resonate in Fortress of Saint John. **Translation** Ho-Kyoon Ahn

Les jardins de la colline. It represents the great Mediterranean tradition of agriculture, forestry and ranching.

©Agence APS

마르세유 연안 지역에서 거대한 도심 재활성화 프로젝트가 활발하게 진행되고 있다. 도시와 바다 사이, J4의 옛 부두 위에 유럽과 지중해 문명 박물관이 수평적인 볼륨을 드러냈다. 이 박물관의 '수직적 성채'는 생-장요새와 대화하고자 하는 열망의 표현이다. 요새의 높은 외벽에 위치한 프로젝트는 수용적 태도를 통해 대상지에서 프로그램을 끌어내는 것이 중요했다. 감각적이고 변증법적인 정원은 그 안에서 자연사 혹은 인간의 역사를 드러내는 지식의 근거를 발견하기 위해 길을 잃어야 하는 '항상 열려 있는 책'으로 간주되었다. 비정형적인 정원의 모습은 그 자체로 시간의 두께를 표현하고 있으며, 정원에서의 산책은 마치 여행의 이야기처럼 각각의 날짜나 이름에 상응하면서 역사를 재구축한다.

사람과 식물의 도착지인 마르세유의 항구에 솟아오른 '이민의 정원'은 지중해 일대 문화의 교류와 이를 통해 이루어진 식물의 교류를 상기시킨다. 연속되는 15점의 그림(정원)은 과시적인 장식이 두드러지는 것을 거부하고 각양각색의 이파리와 질감, 향기로 인한 다양한 감각적 경험에 중점을 둔다. 다양한 통로와 층은 주의 깊은 방문자나 산만한 산책자 모두에게 개화기와 상관없이 일 년 내내 흥미로운 요소를 보장한다. 이는 관리를 크게 필요로 하지 않으며 관수나 시비, 혹은 병충해 방제 처리가 전혀 필요 없는 드라이 가든의 맥락에서 지중해 식물의 식물학적 컬렉션에 가치를 부여한다.

Le parcours ethnobotanique des plantes emblématiques de la méditerranée

©Agence APS

The long flower garden is the fresco of the immense history told by those plants.

15개의 정원-산책로

정원-산책로는 15개의 그림을 전개한다.

1. 오렌지나무 정원: 지중해의 이미지, 무와히드 왕조(12세기에 세워진 베르베르 인과 무슬림 왕조. 북아프리카부터 이베리아 반도까지 지배했고. 코르도바와 세비야도 이들의 영토였다) 정원의 첫 번째 안뜰, 코르도바 혹은 세비야 대 모스크의 오렌지나무 정원의 이미지를 연상시킨다.

2. 도금양 정원: 꽃과 이파리에서 섬세한 향기가 나고, 그 이름이 항상 그라나다의 알함브라를 상기시키는 작은 도금양정원. 도금양과 석류나무로 경계를 두른 직사각형 소로가 있는 엄격한 디자인은 이제는 사라진 총독의 위용을 드러내는 화려한 정원을 상기시킨다.

3. 요새의 야생 풀: 가혹한 환경의 시련을 극복하고 재정복한 식물들에 대해 일종의 경의를 표하는 공간이다. 폐허와 같은 환경에서 저절로 싹을 틔우는 풀들을 위한 정원이다.

4. 높은 곳에 놓인 무화과나무: 무화과나무는 지중해 지역의 상징적인 나무이므로 이곳의 좌대 위에 놓인 것은 매우 자연스럽다. 쉬지 않고 계속 열매를 맺는 이 나무는 지중해의 여러 문화에서 풍요로움의 상징이 되었다.

5. 향초香草의 길: 지중해 요리에 항상 들어가는 허브는 자연스럽게 채원 옆에 자리 잡았다. 손 높이에 식재된 향기 정원은 만져보고 싶은 욕구를 불러일으킨다. 타임, 세이지, 사리에트, 마조람, 라벤더, 히솝 등으로 구성되었다.

5-1. 가시덤불의 향기: 황무지에서 자라는 덤불 식물 중에는 향기가 나는 게 많다(약 10% 종에 향기가 있다고 알려져 있다). 지중해 지역의 공기에는 이 향기가 각인되어 있다. 이는 이 작은 정원이 헌정되어야 할 충분한 이유가 된다.

6. 지중해 채원: 채원은 지중해 채소, 겨울과 여름의 채원, 토종 야채와 지중해의 '전통적인' 요리의 상징이 된 이국 채소의 서사시—'라타투이' 혹은 '보헤미안' 이야기 등—를 이야기한다.

7. 바람의 정원: 화본과禾本科 식물이 가득한 이 정원은, 이 풀들의 우아한 움직임이 바람을 연상케 하고 이주하는 식물들이 씨를 뿌리는 전략에 대해 이야기할 기회를 제공한다.

8. 타작마당: 북서쪽을 향해, 미스트랄(프랑스 남부 지방의 북풍)에 열려있는 타작마당은 바람과 양이 경관의 역동성의 주인공인 크로(프로방스 지방의 자갈 땅)의 대초원, 혹은 라르작(도르도뉴에 위치한 코뮌)의 고원 같은 인근의 다른 경관의 이미지를 반영한다.

9. 언덕의 정원: 여기 가시덤불에서 프랑스 미디 지역의 상징적인 이미지인 마르세유의 언덕과 그곳의 식생, 그리고 무엇보다도 지중해의 농업·임업·목축업의 위대한 전통을 보여준다. 모자이크 경관은 인간에 의한 것이기도 하지만 5천 년 이전부터 불이 만들어낸 것이기도 하다.

10. 털가시나무 총림: 숲을 떠올리지 않고 지중해의 경관을 말하는 것은 불가능하다. 여기에서 숲은 내부분 털가시나무로 채워지는데, 모든 종류의 오븐을 가동하는데 필요한 에너지를 생산하는 이 나무의 용도는 잡목림의 확장을 조장했다. 이제 내일의 지중해 숲의 미래는 어떠할 것인가?

Le jardin des myrtes and Gallery of shadow

Les jardins de la colline

11. 지중해의 상징적인 식물의 인류-식물학적 여정: 지중해의 거대한 인류-식물학 역사는 산책에서 최고조를 이룬다. 이슬람과 유대-기독교 문화 속에서의 식물의 전통적인 사용에 대한 시선의 교차를 볼 수 있다. 식물들이 이야기하는 거대한 역사의 프레스코 그림이 정원의 기다란 화단에 펼쳐진다.

12. 성 요한의 풀: 성聖 요한(생–장)의 허브 정원에 있는 '치유의 풀'들은 세례 요한이 태어난 6월 24일 새벽에 채집한 것이다. 요새의 이름도 이 성인의 이름에서 딴 것이다.

13. 가죽나무 정원: 이곳에 솟아오른 가죽나무 정원은 이국 식물의 도입에 잠재된 문제를 환기하기 위한 것이다.

14. 마와 풀의 정원: 이 정원의 조망은 도시, 그리고 마麻로 향한다. 이는 마르세유 같은 항구에서의 밧줄과 에스파트르(벼과의 다년생 초본, 부드럽고 강인한 섬유질의 줄기로 선박용 밧줄 등을 만든다) 제품의 중요성을 마와 프로방스 지방에서 마 대신에 사용하는 풀(밧줄이나 돗자리를 만드는 화본과 식물)을 통해 말하는 기회다.

15. 마르세유 산업의 정원: 르네 왕의 안뜰의 높은 테라스에서 산책을 완성하면서 식물, 그리고 마르세유와 지중해 산업의 기억이 상기된다. 또한 향료, 커피, 오일, 비누, 아니스 향료, 면직물, 염료 등의 상업의 역사도 정원의 중심에 자리 잡을 것이다.

미래를 향한 정원

이민의 정원은 토종 식물과 외래 식물의 대립을 넘어 투과, 흐름, 이민, 진화의 개념을 숙고하도록 한다. 현대의 유럽과 지중해의 생태적 보고, 식물, 그리고 이와 연관된 활동은 우리가 공유하는 역사를 우리에게 증명하는 지식, 노하우, 방법, 존재의 비정형적 기억을 지원한다.

과거의 이민은 미래의 이민에 대한 질문을 던진다. 과거에 비해 인간의 이동은 더욱 많아지고 그 속도는 점점 더 빨라지고 있다. 그리고 인간의 활동은 경관에 새겨진다. 지구 온난화와 같은 기후변화는 식물의 이주에 어떤 영향을 미칠까? 내일의 자연 환경은 무엇을 닮게 될까? 우리의 문화 경관은 때로는 침략으로 여겨지는 새로운 식물의 도래를 어떻게 통합할까? 이러한 질문은 모두 생-장 요새에서 의미를 지닌다. **번역** 황주영

Garden of Migration leads us to contemplate on permeability, flow, immigration and evolution that lie beneath the conflict for survival between native plants and foreign ones.

©Agence Lumière

23

Guillermo Vázquez Consuegra arquitecto

Jardines del
Hospital en Valencia

Architect Guillermo Vázquez
Consuegra(documentation & direction of
works)
Technical Architect Marcos Vázquez
Consuegra, Javier Estelles
Collaborator Romeck Kruszewski, Gabriel
Verd, Pedro Lara y Alberto Altini, Kristian
Solaun y Elena Vilches(documentation)
Juan José Baena, Teresa Galí
(direction of works)
Structure Eduardo Martínez Moya
(Edartec Consultores)
Service Insur-JG, S.L.
Contractor Midascon(1st phase),
Comsa-Elecnor(2nd phase)
Client Diputación de Valencia(1st phase),
Conselleria d'obres Publiques, Urbanisme
i Transports-Generalitat Valenciana(2nd
phase)
Location Valencia, Spain
Area 26,320m²(1st phase: 8,720m²,
2nd phase: 17,600m²)
Total Cost 4,857,131euro
Documentation
1999(1st phase), 2006(2nd phase)
Construction
2001(1st phase), 2009~2013(2nd phase)
Photographs Alfonso Legaz, David
Frutos, David Zarzoso, Guillermo Vázquez,
Consuegra arquitecto

Elements that remained after the demolition of the whole hospital and medical school in 1963

Recovered elements in our proposal

Existing trees

Newly planted trees

Master plan of 1749

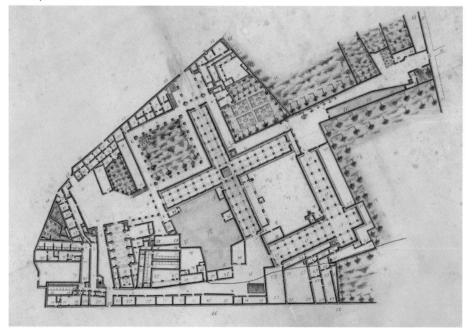

The project for the reorganization of the existing gardens of Hospital is set on the central idea of giving a unified treatment to the entire garden area, built on the site resulting from the demolition, in 1974, of the Hospital de los Pobres Inocentes, important example of hospital complex, whose history goes back to the early fifteenth century. Only the transept of the old nursing, the Capitulet and the little Chapel of Santa Lucia(XVI~XVIII), linked since the beginning to the hospital, survived to the demolition of the complex.

Before the reorganization of the existing gardens of Hospital

The existing gardens are located at a slightly elevated level of the street, which corresponds to the first line of stone blocks of the Hospital that was not removed. A system of earthen paths, with staggered geometry defines different areas where trees of different species and archaeological remains scattered everywhere characterize this green space. The deterioration of the actual conditions and the recent construction of the Museum of Illustration suggest an overall renovation of the whole garden that would highlights how these open spaces are the result of the demolition of the old hospital building and the existing buildings are only fragments of the demolished hospital complex.

The renovation basically proposes flooring in only one material organized on a grid. A tapestry, consisting of small pieces of basalt will lay out on Cartesian geometry that takes its axis from the main piece of the gardens: the transept of the old nursing, nowadays converted into public library.

Over this carpet will appear sunken areas: one of them, without vegetation, will become an orchard of orange trees, safe area where will find accommodation all the archaeological remains, once scattered throughout the landscaped area. The project also involves other archaeological interventions. Especially the ancient church of the Hospital, bigger than the neighboring church of Santa Lucia. The proposal includes the excavation of its archaeological remains to the depth suggested by his foundation and the reorganization of the interior space as an area of gardens. Sunken and shady spaces, protected from heavy traffic in the area, under the big crowns of the trees.

Orchard of orange trees

Orange Square stairs can be a resting place for visitors.

Section of exhibition stand(AA')

Orange Square floor plan

type A

type B

type C

type D

type E

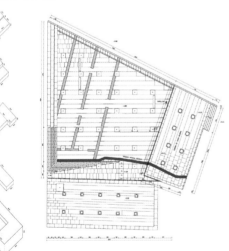

Section of Orange Square(BB')

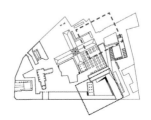

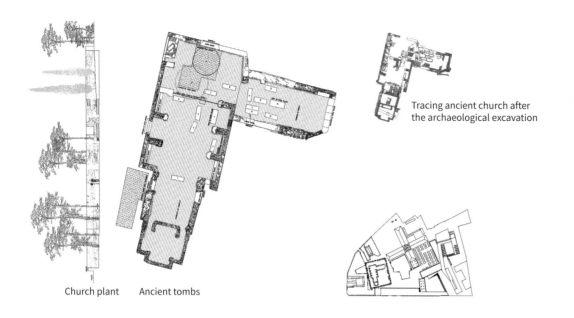

Tracing ancient church after the archaeological excavation

Church plant   Ancient tombs

Accommodation for all the archaeological remains, once scattered throughout the landscaped area.

©David Zarzoso

The proposal maintains the actual level of the garden so that accesses still occur through existing doorways, now covered by steel frame pergola that will contribute to lead to the interior of the garden. In addition are proposed two new entrances, one next to the new Museum of Illustration, demolishing small residual spaces and walls and another, the most important, from the street Hospital. It is an access to the gardens and the Library as well.

The proposal includes the excavation of its archaeological remains.

©David Zarzoso

A soft and wide ramp connects the level of flooring and the garden indoors. Over this ramp
have been placed the intact columns which remain from the old rooms of the Hospital, a new
outdoor hall with 24 columns. The visitor enters the garden through this sloping room, where a
grid of stone columns formalize this new lobby, thus diverting the actual access through the old
Gothic doorway of the Hospital.

Green outdoor rooms, children's playgrounds, metal skins covered with climbing plants for the
irrelevant lateral facades of the Capitulet or the presence of an area enclosed by ponds and
brightly colored flowers, are others of the many ways designed to provide diversified spaces
within new unitary condition of archaeological gardens of the Hospital.

©David Frutos

The project also involves other archaeological interventions.
Especially the ancient church of the Hospital, bigger than the neighboring church of Santa Lucia.

©David Frutos

©David Zarzoso

Existing doorways are now covered by steel frame pergola.

New pergola will contribute to lead to the interior of the garden.

한때는 병원 단지였지만 현재 발렌시아의 주요 공공 도서관으로 이용되고 있는 '발렌시아 공공 도서관'의 기존 정원을 재정비하는 이 프로젝트의 가장 큰 목표는 정원 전체 구역을 통합적으로 구성하는 것이다. 이 정원은 무려 15세기 초에 세워진 스페인의 주요 종합 병원 단지 중 한 곳이었던 오스피탈 데 로 포브레스 이노센테스가 1974년 철거된 자리에 조성되었다. 병원 단지가 철거된 자리에는 병원 건물의 익랑(현재는 공공 도서관으로 이용), 병원 경내 예배당, 15세기 초 병원이 초창기에 연결되어 있던 16~18세기의 작은 산타루치아 성당만이 남아 있었다.

기존 정원은 보행로보다 약간 높은 곳에 위치하고 있기 때문에 철거되지 않은 병원 건물의 판석과 맞닿아 있었다. 정원에 식재된 서로 다른 종의 나무와 곳곳에 산재한 고고학적 유산들이 장소의 개성을 보여주고 기하학적 형태의 흙길이 외부와 정원의 경계를 표시하고 있었다. 그러나 최근 정원의 보존 상태가 악화되고 정원 주변에 일러스트 박물관이 세워짐에 따라 정원에 전반적인 개선 작업이 필요하다는 의견이 제시되었다. 정원의 개선 작업 과정에서 크게 두 가지 사항이 강조되었는데, 먼저 정원을 포함한 이 오픈스페이스가 오래된 병원 건물이 철거된 장소라는 점과 현재의 건물들도 철거된 병원 건물의 일부분이라는 점이다.

Restoration plan for pergola

A tapestry, consisting of small pieces of basalt will lay out on Cartesian geometry that takes its axis from the main piece of the gardens.

하르디네스 델 로스피탈 엔 발렌시아는 한 가지 재료를 사용하여 바닥을 그리드 형태로 조직하면서 정원 개선 작업을 시작했다. 작은 현무암 조각으로 만든 바닥 포장재가 일종의 태피스트리처럼 기하학 형태로 배치되었으며 정원의 중심축을 구성한다. 정원의 선큰 구역 역시 바닥을 잔디 등으로 덮지 않고 태피스트리 카펫으로 포장했다. 이곳은 오렌지나무 광장으로 꾸며지며 정원 전체에 산재해 있던 고고학적 유산들을 모두 수용할 수 있는 안전한 구역으로 이용된다.

산타루치아 성당보다 규모가 더 큼에도 불구하고 오랫동안 방치되어 있던 병원 성당 유적에 대한 고고학적인 개입도 이루어진다. 정원 설계안에서 병원 부지 아래에 묻혀 있던 고고학적 유산들을 발굴하고, 이들 내부 공간을 재조직하여 정원의 일부로 사용하는 안을 제시했다. 정원 내부의 그늘진 선큰 구역은 해당 지역의 극심한 교통 체증으로부터 보호하기 위해 정원에 그늘을 드리운 거대한 나무 아래 위치한다.

정원의 실제 레벨을 그대로 유지하여 기존 정원 출입구를 통해 드나들 수 있게 설계했다. 파사드만 남아 있던 입구에 철골 구조의 퍼걸러를 만들어 보강해 정원 내부로 들어가는 길을 만들었다. 또한 새롭게 만들어진 이 두 개의 출입구 외에 또 하나의 새 출입구가 일러스트 박물관 옆쪽에 있는데 이곳은 이전 병원 건물의 잔여 공간과 벽면 등을 철거하고 세워진 출입구라는 점에서 중요하다. 현재 이 출입문은 정원과 공공 도서관으로 연결된다.

©David Zarzoso

©David Zarzoso

Resting area next to the new outdoor hall with 24 columns

©Guillermo Vázquez Consuegra arquitecto

The visitor enters the garden through the new outdoor hall, where a grid of stone columns formalize
this new lobby, thus diverting the actual access through the old Gothic doorway of the Hospital.

©David Frutos

또한 완만하고 폭이 넓은 경사로가 보행로보다 약간 높은 곳에 위치한 정원과 그 내부를 연결해주고 있다. 정원 내부로 연결되는 이 경사로는 오래전 병원 건물이 있던 터에 온전한 형태로 남겨진 기둥들 사이로 연결된다. 이 곳은 현재 총 24개의 기둥이 세워져 있는 새로운 야외 공간으로 조성되었다. 정원 방문객은 이 경사진 공간을 통해 정원 안으로 들어가게 된다. 격자로 놓인 기둥들이 새로운 정원의 로비 역할을 하며 방문객의 발걸음을 고딕 양식의 병원 출입구로 옮기게 한다.

이외에도 야외의 녹지 공간이나 어린이 놀이 공간, 옛 병원 단지의 유적과는 다소 어울리지 않는 덩굴 식물로 뒤덮인 금속 표면의 화단, 연못과 화려한 색의 꽃으로 둘러싸인 구역 등이 조성되었다. 변화가 많고 다양한 여러 공간을 통합적으로 구성하기 위해 다양한 설계 방식을 적용했다. **번역** 손은신

Atelier Jacqueline Osty & associés

Martin Luther King Park

Design Atelier Jacqueline Osty & associés
Project Team Jérôme Saint-Chély(1st
phase), Daniela Correia with Fanny Sire(2nd
phase)
Association with
François Grether(urban architect),
Concepto(lighting concept), OGI(civil
engineers)
Client City of Paris; DEVE of Paris(Direction
des Espaces Verts et de l'Environnement)
Program Design of an Urban Park in the
Clichy-Batignolles District of Paris
Location Paris, France
Area 4.3ha(1st phase), 5.7ha(2nd phase)
Planning 2005~2006(1st phase),
2008~2011(2nd phase)
Completion 2007(1st phase), 2012~2014
(2nd phase, 1st part), 2017~2020(2nd phase,
2nd part)
Photographs PBA, Dubios Fresney, Martin
Argyroglo, Atelier Jacqueline Osty & associés

Martin Luther King Park is an integral part of the great Clichy-Batignolles urban project, in progress since 2003 and designed by our urban project management team:
J. Osty landscape practice, François Grether practice, urbanists, and OGI, engineers. During the initial study stage, the site was selected to house the Olympic Village, at a time when Paris was a candidate city for the 2012 Olympic Games. Since then, the project has kept most of its main guiding lines.

Prior to the design of this district, the first objective was to clear as much open ground as possible, to plant trees or to lay the foundations of buildings. With that in mind, the railway premises were compacted and limited to the bare essentials for the running of trains. The second objective is to create a park from which a new district will emerge, espousing the city limits, meshing with future urban forms and connecting the already existing adjoining green areas. The third objective is to connect he various districts that lie from north to south and east to west of the park by means of an orthogonal system matching the Batignolles District's

2007	2014	2020	

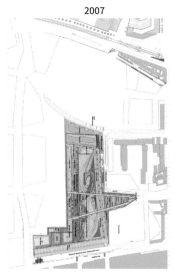   

1st part realized(4ha)	2nd part phase 1 realized	2nd part phase 2	Park in the long term

Past of the site

Future of the site

orthogonal grid. This set up will be crossed diagonally by 600 meters long alley, directly connecting the district and its old urban garden with Porte de Clichy. With its tree-lined walks, the lay-out prolongs the city and its urban axes within the park.

The project is directed by the site's heritage as much as by the present or future elements around it. Overall, the park keeps the artificial topography of the railway embankment, a horizontal one as compared to the natural slope of the north-oriented watershed of the Seine River. On the western side, leveling structures, such as esplanades, terraces and ramps are used to cross over the St. Lazare network and to interconnect the districts.

A heritage element, a witness to railway history, the "Petite Ceinture(small ring railway)," is both kept at a distance and enhanced by a large pond located right in the center of the park. On the eastern side, the railway can be crossed by means of stairs and lifts integrated within a Belvedere building.

The geometry of the park, in long stretches, reflects the direction of the railway lines, parallel to the main rail network and perpendicular to Cardinet Street, to the south. The design of stretches offers a strategic advantage for the cultivation and organization of diversity. Each of the them has its own style and function, offering varied emotional experiences of space, whether one follows long, straight walks on flat ground, or curved paths closely fitting the relief of a landscaped rather than functional topography. Throughout the park, 3 themes are developed in a contemporary type of plurality and evolving approach.

The geometry of the park, in long stretches, reflects the direction of the railway lines, parallel to the main rail network and perpendicular to Cardinet Street, to the south.

The new building going above the "Petite Ceinture." The park is divided in two by the Petite Ceinture, railway going all around Paris, unused today. This new building allows the pedestrian to go above it. It is also a cafe.

Body and Space

With its wide open spaces, like the two large lawns on either side of the ponds, with more intimate areas, such as the Belvedere walks, with action areas dedicated to children's games and the sports facilities characteristic of new urban esthetics, the park offers a great variety of uses in keeping with contemporary expectations. The large number of visitors vouches for that. Everybody can make use of the park as they wish, sitting or running, playing or strolling around, picnicking or daydreaming, enjoying peace or the company of others, seeing or being seen, being an actor or a spectator.

The Show of Seasons

Plants, the core matter of the park, are of utmost importance: throughout the year, a wealth of species provides a jubilating renewal of sights. The cycle of seasons promotes the creation of vegetal happenings in the park. It has guided the choice of plantations, ensuring that from south to north, a particular season is highlighted: the flowering of cherry and magnolia trees, and the interplay of light and shadows in the spring, the lawns and grasses of summer, the glorious foliage of fall and the bark of birch groves and pine trees of winter.

The soft ground drawing is a reference to the running tracks. The park was originally to become the Olympic Village if Paris had won the Games in 2012.

Skatepark

©Dubois Fresney

The summer area of the park during autumn. The park is divided in season areas where the season dedicated to each part is highlighted by a vegetation palette which enhanced that season, but the office looked into having all this parts work all year long also.

©Martin Argyroglo

49

Water in All Its Forms

Water management installs a genuine engineering of living elements. Throughout the park, water takes on a variety of forms: technical, landscaped, environmental or playful. The technical form is expressed in the collection and storage of rainwater, re-used for watering purposes; planted ditches and stone or metal gutters take the collected rainwater into a 1,500m^3 storage tank. During dry periods, a windmill pumps out water from the ponds to maintain moisture in the ditches. At the center of the park, there are 4 biotope ponds covering 9,000m^2, sustained by water from the Seine. It is allowed to settle in the first pond, and is filtered out in the next two ponds. Finally, a monumental waterfall provides oxygen for the water reaching the 4th pond. A playful use of water is offered on the Square of Springs, above the storage tank, for the pleasure of children and adults alike.

The park disseminates between islands of construction on a porosity principle. The aim is to develop a maximum of vistas and visual continuity from the park to the other space open onto the sky: the railway lines. It makes public space green and also the hearts of the constructed islands that are their terraces and balconies. It positions some of the major buildings, like the Hall of Justice, grafted onto the great diagonal axis.

Grand bassin in 2014, seven years after being constructed

마틴 루터 킹 파크는 클리시 바티뇰 도시 개발 프로젝트를 구성하는 핵심적인 부분이다. 이 도시 개발 프로젝트는 2003년 초기 연구 조사 단계에서 굳어진 가이드라인에 따라 진행되었으며, 이는 공원 설계 방향에도 적지 않은 영향을 미쳤다.

이 지구를 계획하기에 앞서, 가장 우선적으로 고려한 것은 나무를 심거나 건물의 기초를 놓기 위해 가능한 많은 땅을 정비하고 다듬어 놓는 것이었다. 이 목표를 염두에 두자, 철로를 위한 부지는 좁아졌고 기차를 운영하는데 필요한 최소한의 필지만이 남게 되었다. 두 번째 목표는 도시 경계를 유지함과 동시에 미래의 도시 형태와 이미 형성되어 있는 주변의 녹지를 한데 연결시켜줌으로써 새로운 바티뇰을 위한 공원을 조성하는 것이었다. 세 번째 목표는 바티뇰 지구에 도입되는 그리드에 상응하는 직교 체계를 통해 공원의 북쪽에서 남쪽으로, 서쪽에서 동쪽으로 자리하고 있는 여러 지구를 연결하는 것이었다.

마틴 루터 킹 파크는 전반적으로 철로를 놓기 위해 축조되었던 인공 지형 위에 놓여 있다. 이 지형은 북쪽을 향해 흐르는 센 강 유역에 자연적으로 발생한 경사면에 비해 비교적 수평에 가까운 편이다. 서쪽으로는 산책로와 테라스, 경사로와 같이 단차를 극복하기 위한 요소를 도입했고, 생 라자르 철도 네트워크를 가로지르며 대상지에 인접한 지구를 서로 연결시킬 수 있도록 했다.

The wet ditch, part of the water system of the park

길게 뻗어 있는 공원의 기하학적 형상은 철로의 흔적을 반영하고 있다. 이러한 형상은 주된 철도 노선과는 평행을 이루고, 대상지 남쪽의 카르디네 거리와는 수직을 이룬다. 대상지를 길게 뻗은 형태로 구성함으로써 공간이 가질 수 있는 다양성을 체계적으로 수용하고 조직할 수 있는 전략적 이점을 얻으려 했다. 각 공간은 그 고유한 구성 방식과 기능을 갖추고 있으며, 다양한 공간 체험을 감성적으로 제공한다. 평평한 땅 위로 길고 곧게 뻗은 길을 따라 걷거나, 조경이 강조된 지형에 따라 구불구불하게 형성된 길을 따라 걸으며 공원을 감상할 수 있다. 이러한 기하학적 골격에 더해 다원성을 고려한 점진적인 접근 방식이 도입되었고, 그에 따라 다음과 같은 세 가지 성격을 가진 공간이 조성되었다.

A playful use of water is offered on the Square of Springs, above the storage tank, for the pleasure of children and adults alike.

The dry fountain

신체와 공간

마틴 루터 킹 파크는 연못 양쪽에 자리한 잔디밭과 같은 넓은 오픈스페이스, 전망대 길과 같은 친숙하고 아기자기하게 꾸며진 구역, 아이들의 놀이 공간, 그리고 현재는 스포츠 공간으로 활용되고 있는 액션 구역 등을 갖추고 있다. 누구든지 자신이 원하는 방식으로 공원을 이용할 수 있다. 곳곳에 배치된 벤치에 앉아 있거나 길게 뻗어있는 길을 따라 달릴 수도 있다. 놀이를 하거나 산책을 할 수 있고, 넓은 잔디밭에서 소풍을 즐기거나 몽상에 젖을 수도 있다. 한가로운 일상을 즐기거나 새로운 사람을 사귈 수도 있고, 누군가를 바라보고 또 누군가가 바라보는 대상이 됨으로써 배우가 될 수도, 관람객이 될 수도 있다.

사계절의 표현

공원의 사계절을 표현하는 데 있어 식물은 무엇보다 중요한 요소다. 일 년 내내 풍부한 수종을 유지하여 늘 새롭고 멋진 모습을 연출하는 것이다. 계절의 변화에 따라 공원에서는 식물의 향연이 더욱 다채롭게 펼쳐진다. 특정 주제에 따라, 남쪽에서부터 북쪽에 이르기까지 각 계절을 강조할 수 있도록 식생을 선택했다. 즉 봄에는 벚꽃과 목련꽃을 피워 빛과 그림자의 상호 작용을 기대했고, 여름에는 초록의 잔디와 풀, 가을에는 빛나는 단풍잎, 겨울에는 소나무와 자작나무의 수피가 보여주는 아름다움을 표현하려 했다.

©Dubios Fresney

The park conception tries to give space to all type of activities. Martin Luter King Park makes public space green and also the hearts of the constructed islands that are their terraces and balconies.

다양한 물의 형태

물을 관리한다는 것은 살아 있는 요소를 다루는 진정한 의미의 설비 공학을 의미한다. 공원에서 사용되는 물에는 화장실 등에서 쓰이는 공원 운영 용수, 조경 용수, 놀이를 위한 물 등이 포함된다. 공원 운영 용수는 우수의 저장, 중수 처리 등을 통해 축적된다. 식재된 배수로와 돌, 금속 홈통을 통해 집수되고 1,500m³의 저장 탱크를 채우게 된다. 건기에는 풍차를 통해 연못에서부터 물을 퍼 올림으로써 배수로의 습기를 유지한다.

물이 흥미를 끄는 요소로 활용되는 경우는 저장 탱크 위에 있는 '샘물 광장'에서 발견할 수 있다. 샘물 광장은 아이들뿐만 아니라 어른들도 좋은 시간을 보낼 수 있는 규모다. 공원 중앙에는 센 강의 물로 유지되는 총 9,000m² 면적에 달하는 네 곳의 생태 연못이 있다. 우선 첫 번째 연못에 강물이 저장되고, 이렇게 저장된 물은 그 옆의 다른 두 연못에서 정화된다. 정화 과정을 거친 물은 마지막으로 네 번째 연못으로 흘러들어가고 이곳의 폭포를 통해 산소를 제공받는다.

이 공원은 건축적 섬들 사이사이를 다공성의 원리에 따라 침투하는 형상을 보여준다. 재판소와 같은 몇몇 대표적 건물들을 한 데 엮어내 거대한 사선 축을 이루고 있고, 공원에서부터 다른 오픈스페이스를 거쳐 하늘까지 이어지는 시각적 연속성과 탁 트인 조망을 확보한다. 마틴 루터 킹 파크는 기존 공공 공간에 더 많은 녹지를 제공하면서 건축물의 테라스와 발코니로 기능한다. **번역** 우영선

West 8

Maxima Park

Landscape Architects West 8
Client Project Development Leidsche Rijn
Location Utrecht, The Netherlands
Design 1997~2013
Realisation 2005~2014
Size 300ha
Photographs West 8, Eva S Andersson,
Jeroen Musch, Johan de Boer

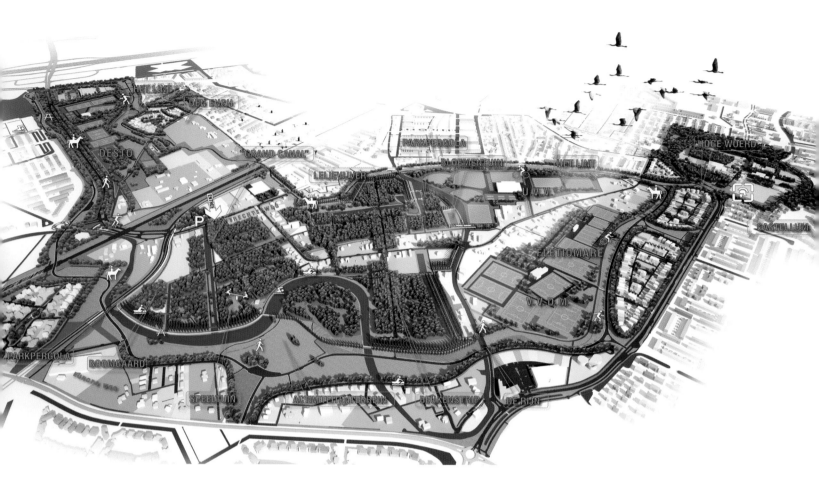

The design for Maxima Park, formerly Leidsche Rijn Park, was the outcome of a design competition held in 1997. The concept for the park, to be constructed in a new residential district of 35,000 homes to the west of Utrecht, is based on creating three "edges" that shield the park from its suburban surroundings.

The edges consist of a re-excavated former meander of the River Vikingrhine, a 9km long ecological zone and a 3.5km long pergola around the core of the park. The core is a 50ha green courtyard, called "Binnenhos." It contains woods, water courses, pedestrian areas, playground and formal avenues which create a secluded green inner world that can be entered only through gateways. The surrounding six meter high pergola is a fauna wall, which will attract all kinds of animals and plants, thus creating its own ecosystem.

Surrounding the core are sports fields, allotments and other facilities which are linked by a linear park of flowery meadows. Hikers, cyclists and skaters can move through this circuit park over a track that offers them constantly changing perspectives.

The park is essential to counterbalance the inescapable sea of houses and puts its mono-functional character into perspective. Above all the park will offer a factor of growth. With its consciously chosen long-term life cycle it will grow beyond the eternal youth of the suburban environment.

Het Lint

The Lint is generally 30m wide with a fringe of forest(15m) on the outer side, which loops around the entire park area. The meadows in the inside of the Lint are free of obstacles. The long route on the Lint gives users varying perspectives on sports fields, gardens, the green middle area, water, natural forest and the lake. The Lint can also be used for recreational activities, sports, walking and to enjoy nature. In the middle the Lint has a 6m asphalt path called the "track," which is bordered by concrete curb stones that are embossed with a delicate flower motif.

The Lint is an important structural element and is essential for the functioning of the park. It provides access from the surrounding residential areas and it connects the numerous facilities in the park. The Lint, also has a more figurative function, it provides the park with a narrative, encompassing the biography of the area in one route and displaying both ecological and cultural dimensions. The lint is the key ecological link between adjacent natural areas. Alternately water, river, grassland, pasture, brush and trees exist on the Lint, this diversity offers habitats for a variety of flora and fauna.

Pavilion

West 8 designed a new pavilion, inspired by the never realized design by one of Holland's most famous architects Cuijpers, as part of the design for Maxima Park. The pavilion or teahouse has become a place to relax with family and friends, after a long walk through the lush green park or a boat trip on the Vikingrhine.

The pavilion has become a place to relax with family and friends.

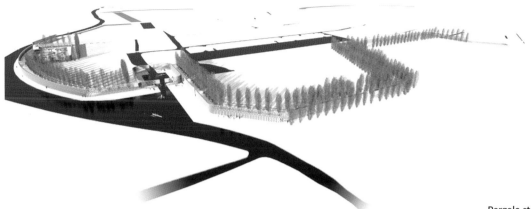

Pergola structures

The pergola serves both an ecological and botanical function within the park program.

Climbing plants will be planted at the base of every column.

Pergola

In the early stage of the design process for Maxima Park it was decided that the most frequently visited and central part of the Park should be framed with an iconic pergola. This decision resulted in the creation of the "Binnenhof" Courtyard and the distinctive Park Pergola. The Municipality of Utrecht insisted that these two park elements must meet a high set of standards regarding sustainability, visual quality, maintenance and have a life span of a 100 years. The route and building height of the Park Pergola were also fixed in the zoning plan. The technical and architectural design was created to meet these preconditions and subsequently permission was granted to procure and construct the first kilometer of the pergola. Over the course of the upcoming winter/spring season the first phase of the pergola will be completed and climbing plants will be planted at the base of every column.

Cutting Edge Structural Performance

Unlike other pergola structures made of wood, wood and brickwork, steel, netting or steel cables, this six meter high pergola is designed as individual but interchangeable precast concrete element that can be combined to form a cohesive structure. The advantages of concrete in terms of durability and repetition have been fully exploited and the material's possibilities with respect to its sculptural qualities—curves, facets, shadow, texture, relief and embossing work have also been explored at length. By working extensively on molding and casting techniques and devoting careful attention to the

By using both inner and outer curved elements the pergola can wind through old plot patterns and woodlands.

quality of the construction during manufacturing, the limits concerning concrete finishing and density were sought. The resulting precast elements are very slim and extremely graceful. The pergola's silky smooth finish and striking white color make it soft and touchable, like ivory. Apart from the standard elements(600 x 330 x 80cm; 3.5tons), curved elements have also been custom designed and manufactured. As a result the pergola does not follow a straight line or a square shape. By using both inner and outer curved elements the pergola can wind through old plot patterns and woodlands. The visitor never gets to see the beginning nor the end, as the structure continually disappears from one's perspective. The curved elements also take on a very sculptural quality because the honeycomb structure appears to rotate in the light.

Front and Backside

Although the Park Pergola is currently naked in time it will be overgrown with a verdant cloak of climbing plants along its entire length. Winding vines will climb onto the smooth side of the Park Pergola. While the coarser concrete texture on the inner side of the Park Pergola, a result of a lava stone additive, will encourage the growth of epiphytic plants, moss and sedum. The legibility of the "Inside" and "Outside" of the pergola will help park visitors to orient themselves.

Ecology and Participation

The pergola functions as a veil that is drawn around the "Binnenhof" Courtyard. The legs form gates inviting the visitor to enter anywhere they please. Historical parks have gates and walls. This park shares the same tradition of enclosure and feeling of "being insides," but adopts a more democratic approach: you can enter anywhere. Some of the legs have a small protrusion which can be used as seating.

The pergola serves both an ecological and botanical function within the park program as large collections of climbing plants have been planted along the base of the pergola. Near the Lily Pond a section of the pergola has been specifically been designated for rich flowering species, while other parts are more "quiet" to create ecological differentiation. In the "quieter" areas the honeycomb structure acts as a frame in which special bat boxes, nesting boxes for owls and substrate bins for rare wall vegetation(ferns) will be placed. School groups and the "Friends of the Maxima Park" association will participate in maintenance of these bins and boxes.

Concrete curb stones that are embossed with a delicate flower motif.

©Jeroen Musch

Hikers, cyclists and skaters can move through this circuit park over a track that offers them constantly changing perspectives.

©Johan de Boer

과거 레이쉬 레인 파크라는 이름으로 불렸던 막시마 파크의 설계는 1997년 개최된 디자인 공모전의 결과물이다. 위트레흐트 서부 지역에 건설될 3만5천 가구 규모의 신규 주거 지역에 조성되는 이 공원의 기본 구상은 주변 지역으로부터 공원을 둘러싸는 이른바 세 개의 '모서리'를 만드는 것을 그 골자로 한다. 이러한 모서리들은 새롭게 만들어진 바이킹라인 강의 곡류 구간, 9km 길이의 생태 지역 그리고 공원 중심부에 자리한 3.5km 길이의 퍼걸러로 구성된다.

공원 중심부는 50헥타르 넓이의 잔디 마당으로 '비넨호프'라는 이름으로 불린다. 이곳에는 숲, 수로, 보행자 구역, 놀이터 그리고 형식을 갖춘 진입로 등이 위치하고 있으며, 그 안쪽으로 자리한 한적한 녹지 공간은 출입구를 통해서만 접근 가능하다. 주위를 둘러싼 6m 높이의 퍼걸러는 온갖 동식물을 끌어들이는 역할을 함으로써 자체적인 생태계를 만들어 낼 것이다.

공원 중심부 주변으로는 운동장, 주말 농장, 기타 시설물들이 자리해, 꽃으로 덮인 초지형 공원을 통해 서로 연결된다. 하이커나 자전거 및 스케이트를 타는 사람들은 별도로 마련된 트랙으로 이동하면서 순환형 공원을 감상하고, 끊임없이 변화하는 다양한 경치를 만끽할 수 있다.

택지 개발을 하면 수많은 주택이 들어서게 되는데, 공원은 그로 인한 부작용을 상쇄하는데 반드시 필요한 시설이다. 또한 공원을 통해 자칫 단조로워질 수 있는 그 지역의 성격을 보완해줄 수 있으며, 무엇보다도 새로운 성장 동력을 얻을 수 있다. 막시마 파크는 세심하게 기획된 장기적 운영 계획 덕분에 교외 지역이 갖는 근본적 성장 한계를 뛰어넘는 발전상을 보여줄 것이다.

헤트 린트

린트는 대개 30m 정도의 폭을 가진다. 바깥쪽으로는 약 15m 정도 되는 띠처럼 늘어선 숲을 갖는 게 보통이며, 공원의 전 영역을 고리 모양으로 감싼다. 린트 내부에 위치한 초지에는 어떠한 장애물도 존재하지 않는다. 방문객들은 린트 위로 길게 뻗은 길을 따라 운동장, 정원, 녹색 중간 지대, 강, 자연림, 호수 등을 다채로운 시각으로 조망할 수 있다. 또한 린트는 다양한 여가 활동, 운동, 산책 등에 적합한 장소일 뿐만 아니라 자연을 느끼기에 안성맞춤인 공간이다. 린트의 중앙부에는 이른바 '트랙'이라 불리는 아스팔트 길이 자리하고 있는데, 섬세한 꽃무늬가 돋을새김으로 장식된 콘크리트 갓돌을 통해 주변과 분리된다.

린트는 공원의 전체적 구조에 있어 매우 중요한 요소이며, 공원이 기능을 제대로 발휘하기 위해 반드시 필요하다. 린트를 통해 주변 주거 지역으로부터의 접근이 용이해지며, 공원 내의 여러 시설들이 한데 연결될 수 있다. 또한 린트는 기능적인 것 이상의 역할을 하는데, 공원 전역에 걸친 생물학적 특성을 하나의 경로를 통해 포괄적으로 보여주는 동시에 생태적·문화적 측면을 부각시켜 공원이 나름의 이야기를 지닐 수 있도록 해주기 때문이다.

린트는 공원과 그 주변을 둘러싼 자연환경을 이어주는 핵심적 연결고리이기도 하다. 강, 초지, 덤불, 나무 등이 린트 위에 앞서거니 뒤서거니 등장하는데, 린트는 이러한 다양성 덕분에 여러 동식물에게 훌륭한 서식지를 제공할 수 있다.

The curvy bridge over the Lelievijver

파빌리온

West 8은 막시마 파크 설계의 한 부분으로 새로운 파빌리온을 디자인했는데, 네덜란드 최고의 건축가 중 한 명인 쿠이퍼스의 작품들 가운데 지금껏 단 한 번도 구체화되지 못했던 디자인에서 영감을 받았다. 찻집으로도 역할하는 파빌리온은 공원에서 장시간 산책한 뒤 혹은 바이킹라인 강에서 뱃놀이를 한 후, 가족 또는 친구들과 편안한 휴식을 취할 수 있는 공간으로 자리 잡았다.

파크 퍼걸러

막시마 파크에서 사람들의 방문이 가장 빈번하고 핵심적인 장소에 상징성이 큰 퍼걸러를 설치하자는 의견이 공원의 초기 설계 단계에 개진되었으며, 이를 반영하기로 결정되었다. 이러한 결정을 토대로 '비넨호프' 코트야드와 독특한 형태의 파크 퍼걸러가 탄생했다.

위트레흐트 시정부 측에서는 공원 건립에 포함된 이 두 가지 시설 모두가 지속가능성, 심미성 그리고 유지·보수 등에 있어 높은 기준을 충족시킬 수 있어야 하며, 100년 이상 갈 수 있어야 한다는 점을 강조했다. 동선과 파크 퍼걸러의 높이 등도 구획을 확정할 때 함께 결정되었다. 이러한 선결 조건을 충족시킬 수 있도록 시공과 건축 설계가 이루어졌으며, 이후 퍼걸러 전체 가운데 첫 1km를 건설해도 좋다는 허가가 났다. 겨울과 봄에 걸쳐 1단계 퍼걸러 공사가 마무리되었으며, 각각의 기둥 밑부분에는 덩굴 식물이 식재됐다.

대개의 퍼걸러 구조물은 목재, 벽돌, 강철, 그물 혹은 강철 케이블 등으로 구성되는 것이 보통이지만, 막시마 파크에 들어선 6m 높이의 퍼걸러는 분리 및 교환 사용이 가능한 블록 성형된 콘크리트 소재로 이루어졌다. 내구성 측면에서 콘크리트가 갖는 장점을 최대한 활용했고, 곡면, 표면, 그림자, 질감, 돋을새김, 부각 등 소재 자체가 지닌 조형적 특성들을 폭넓게 이용했다. 몰딩 및 캐스팅 기술을 십분 활용하고 생산 과정에서 재료의 품질에 대해 세심한 주의를 기울임으로써, 콘크리트 소재의 마감 및 밀도 등과 관련된 기준을 충족할 수 있었다. 이를 통해 확보한 블록 성형된 콘크리트 소재는 매우 얇고, 우아한 모습을 뽐낸다.

생태 및 시민 참여

퍼걸러는 '비넨호프' 코트야드 주변에 드리워진 장막과 같은 역할을 한다. 퍼걸러의 기둥들은 관문을 만들어 방문객들이 원하는 장소로 자유롭게 이동할 수 있도록 돕는다. 유서 깊은 공원에는 이처럼 관문과 벽 등이 있기 마련인데, 막시마 파크 역시 이러한 전통을 이어 '내부에 들어와 있다'는 느낌을 자아낸다. 동시에 보다 민주적인 접근 방법도 도입되었는데, 방문객들이 어디든 아무런 제약 없이 돌아다닐 수 있다는 점이다. 퍼걸러의 몇몇 기둥에는 돌출부를 두어 방문객들이 앉을 수 있도록 했다.

퍼걸러는 공원 전반에 걸친 식생 프로그램의 일환으로 생태적 역할을 하는데, 대규모의 덩굴 식물이 퍼걸러 아래쪽에 식재되어 자라고 있다. 백합 연못 부근에 위치한 퍼걸러의 경우 개화성 식물을 위해 별도의 공간이 마련되어 있는 반면, 여타 지역은 생태적 차별성을 꾀하기 위한 차원에서 보다 '차분한' 성격을 자아낸다. 이 '차분한' 지역에는 벌집 구조물이 일종의 틀 역할을 함으로써 특수 제작한 박쥐용 상자, 올빼미 둥지를 위한 상자, 희귀 벽면 식생을 위한 시설 등이 들어서게 된다. **번역** 안호균

In the middle the Lint has a 6m asphalt path called the "track," which is bordered by concrete curb stones that are embossed with a delicate flower motif.

The visitor never gets to see the beginning nor the end, as the structure continually disappears from one's perspective.

Queen Elizabeth Olympic Park

James Corner Field Operations

Urban Design & Landscape Architecture
James Corner Field Operations
Prime Contractor Skanska
Landscape Contractor Willerby Landscape
Landscape Architect of Record LDA Design
Engineering Services Arup
Cost Estimating Deloitte
Water Feature Design The Fountain Workshop
Event Consultant Groundbreaking
Architecture Make Architects
Planting Design Piet Oudolf
Playground Consultant Play Link
Lighting Design Speirs+Major
Art/Wayfinding Tomato
Irrigation Design Waterwise Solutions
Client London Legacy Development Company
Location London, United Kingdom
Area 22ha
Completion 2014. 4.
Photographs London Legacy Development Corporation, Piet Oudolf, James Corner Field Operations, Robin Forster / LDA Design

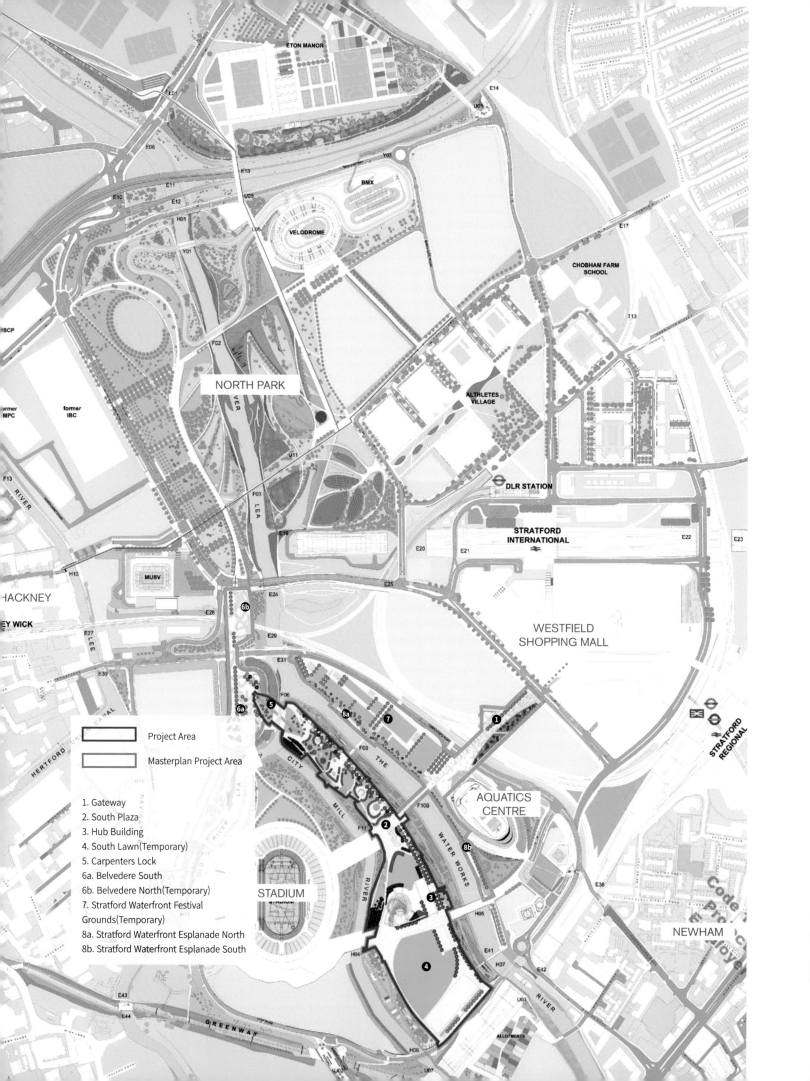

ETON MANOR

BMX

VELODROME

NORTH PARK

CHOBHAM FARM SCHOOL

former MPC

former IBC

ATHLETES VILLAGE

DLR STATION

STRATFORD INTERNATIONAL

HACKNEY

HACKNEY WICK

MUSV

WESTFIELD SHOPPING MALL

STRATFORD REGIONAL

AQUATICS CENTRE

STADIUM

WATER WORKS

NEWHAM

GREENWAY

ALLOTMENTS

Project Area

Masterplan Project Area

1. Gateway
2. South Plaza
3. Hub Building
4. South Lawn(Temporary)
5. Carpenters Lock
6a. Belvedere South
6b. Belvedere North(Temporary)
7. Stratford Waterfront Festival
Grounds(Temporary)
8a. Stratford Waterfront Esplanade North
8b. Stratford Waterfront Esplanade South

Built on the grounds of the London 2012 Olympic Games, South Park at Queen Elizabeth Olympic Park was conceived as a 21st Century Pleasure Garden. Whereas the northern half of Queen Elizabeth Olympic Park is defined by extensive green spaces, vegetated hills and plateaus, nature trails and wetlands, the southern half is defined by its eventfulness, creative programming and attractions. In this way, South Park would build on London's great tradition of pleasure gardens—from Vauxhall and Marylebone, to Ranleigh and Cremorne—each destination parks renowned for their beautiful landscapes, cultural attractions, mystery, dreaminess, surprise and fun.

The Park site, once the centre of industrial invention and innovation, was first transformed into the centerpiece of the London 2012 Olympic Games, and most recently into an extraordinary legacy for the city and a new park typology where new communities are linked to sport, culture, education and their environment. Formerly the expansive hardscape of the Olympic concourse, South Park today unfolds over 22-hectares, surrounded by rivers, canals and spectacular architecture(including Zaha Hadid's swimming hall and Anish Kapoor's ArcelorMittal Orbit).

Four Physical Landscape Frameworks

As the programmatic center of Queen Elizabeth Olympic Park, South Park can be understood through its four physical landscape frameworks, which organize the site and shape a highly social series of "Pleasure Gardens":

The Arc Promenade is the new spine and major social device of South Park—and is intended as a bold connection between the northern and southern areas of the overall site, linking together all of the major spaces and features. Akin to a grand strolling promenade, the arc strongly orients the visitor on the site while establishing open views and connections. The promenade is tree-lined with large formal trees, richly furnished with a range of social furniture, and supports various pavilions, kiosks, and spaces for events, such as linear markets, festivals, and fairs.

Planting Ribbon is a 5m-wide planting strip of young trees, shrubs and tall textural grasses and perennials. It dramatically meanders along the western edge of the Arc Promenade, effectively shaping spaces and "rooms" for socialization and event programming. Openings are carefully located along the ribbon to allow generous passage between the spaces and to coordinate with the site's below grade infrastructure.

The Park site, once the centre of industrial invention and innovation, was first transformed into the centerpiece of the London 2012 Olympic Games.

The Event Rooms are flexible spaces that can support performance functions, public art, programmed events and attractions. The Event Rooms vary in size to meet the Client's brief for the park to accommodate a wide range of events, from large concerts and festivals to small gatherings, exhibition, performances, play and art. Oriented west and south are a series of Lawns and Gardens. These are soft, flexible green spaces for passive uses in contrast to the harder, more active spaces to the east.

Taken together, the Arc Promenade, Planting Ribbon, Event Rooms and the Lawns and Gardens create a powerful landscape for both everyday use and enjoyment, as well as for supporting a wide range of event programming, from food festivals and markets to rides and small circuses, to concerts and performances, to arts, culture and education. The spaces are clearly legible, playful and varied, while at the same time capable of supporting a diverse range of uses. This theatrical event site, set within a larger network of ecological green systems, waterways and world—class attractions, continues to create a destination park for London beyond the Olympics— scenic and social on a daily basis, and eventful and active when programmed.

Design Strategy

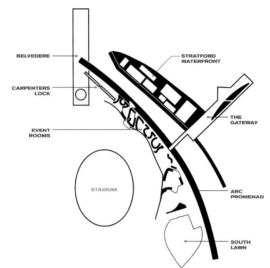

Event Paltforms for South Park

Arc Promenade

Planting Ribbon

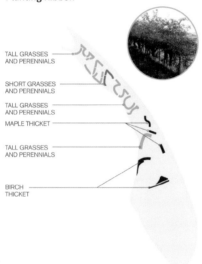

Event Rooms

Lawns & Gardens

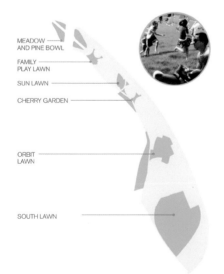

Planting

The Planting Ribbon, which variegated "hedgerow" can in some places be porous and open and in other places dense and enclosing; sometimes grassy and floral; wild and mixed in some areas and thicket-like in others. It's variety in species and structure will enhance the overall habitat range for the Park, supporting birdlife, butterflies and other fauna. As seen from the Orbit, the shaped composition will be a striking and graphic expression of the Pleasure Gardens. Openings are carefully located along the ribbon to allow passage between the spaces and species selection and mixture is coordinated with the site's below-grade infrastructure.

The Arc Promenade will be lined with a double row of large canopy trees to create a majestic shaded promenade. These trees will become more mixed and varied towards the northern end of the site, capturing the transition to the more informal character of the park's North. Flowering Trees are scattered across the "Lawns and Gardens," in coordination with the site's below-grade infrastructure.

Central to the Park's design is the 5m-wide planting strip of young trees, shrubs and tall textural grasses and perennials dramatically meanders along the western edge of the Arc Promenade, effectively shaping spaces and "rooms" for socialization and event programming.

The Water Labyrinth is a continuous linear feature that mimics the form of the "Planting Ribbon," similarly creating a striking visual form as well as a series of "rooms" within the enfolded line.

Furnishings

The furnishings for South Park are designed and organized to encourage a broad range of social interactions. A series of generously dimensioned elements are placed strategically at key locations along the Arc Promenade and within the Event Rooms to further distinguish the Park as a welcoming, social place. The furnishing palette for the Park incorporates elements from the Olympic Games, and expands the timber, metal and concrete palette to accommodate a greater range of furnishing types and configurations. The material selection reinforces the design intent and allows for flexibility of choices as the Park develops over time. The materials are durable and to the extent possible recycled, sustainable and vandal-proof.

Play

The Park has been designed to enable socializing and playful engagement with the public realm as much as possible. The range and type of play opportunities for children and families help ensure an active, social and playful atmosphere for the park—even on unprogrammed or non—event days. The Park integrates a rich mix of spaces, multipurpose features and landscape elements that encourage play for all ages:

The Water Labyrinth is a continuous linear feature that mimics the form of the "Planting Ribbon," similarly creating a striking visual form as well as a series of "rooms" within the enfolded line. The feature consists of a 1.5m wide, flush-to-grade concrete paving strip with water jet nozzles spaces regularly down the centerline. The jets are individually supported by low-voltage submersible pumps, which provide a fantastic degree of control over the individual jets. With the high-degree of control over the jets, there is great potential to provoke interaction and play. A mechanical plant room and holding tank that supports the water feature is located beneath an existing bridge abutment, with access along existing Olympic steps and pathways.

Fun & Playful Furnishings are located along the Arc Promenade. These include timber porch swings, climbable "abacus" ladders and spaces for seating and lounging. Arranged along the eastern edge of the promenade beneath the shade trees and adjacent to the other seating elements and pavilions, the play elements are intended to be flexible and non-prescriptive, accessible and available for all ages.

Play Room is situated within one of the event rooms. With a dramatic red colour theme that (including red acrylic coating on asphalt and red rubberized play surface) and furnished with a field of interactive and playful features (large-scale boulders, bespoke climbing elements, water pump, and various timber play elements) the Play Room is a major draw for the Park, attracting children and families because of its mix of play and risk. The design supports not only climbing but also hiding, swinging, crawling, and jumping. The surfaces within this playroom are a mix of rubber, sand, and grass to provide a variety of places for play for mixed ages as well as rest for families. Parents are invited to sit on the adjacent lawns, on the perimeter benches or in the shade of the promenade.

Since it's opening day in April 2014, the Park is proving to be a catalyst for social, economic and environmental transformation for this neglected part of East London, and helping to revive the Lower Lee Valley region. Certainly the whole idea that this part of the larger ensemble of parks and spaces as active, eventful and capable of absorbing large crowds is very evident. North Park remains serene, beautiful, scenic and "slow" while South Park promotes movement, spectacle, interaction and event.

Play Room is situated within one of the event rooms. With a dramatic red colour theme that (including red acrylic coating on asphalt and red rubberized play surface) and furnished with a field of interactive and playful features.

©James Corner Field Operations

2012 런던 올림픽 게임 부지에 조성된 퀸 엘리자베스 올림픽 파크 사우스 파크는 21세기의 플레저 가든으로 계획되었다. 퀸 엘리자베스 올림픽 파크의 북쪽 절반이 방대한 녹지, 식재된 언덕과 언덕 위 평지, 자연형 산책로와 습지로 계획된 반면, 남쪽 절반(사우스 파크)은 다양한 이벤트, 창의적인 프로그램과 사람들을 끌어들이는 명소로 계획되었다. 그 결과 사우스 파크는 복스홀과 매릴번에서부터 랜레이 그리고 크레몬으로 이어지는 런던 고유의 플레저 가든이라는 훌륭한 전통을 바탕으로 지어지게 되었다.

한때 산업적인 발명과 혁신의 중심지였던 공원 부지는 먼저 2012년 런던 올림픽 게임의 중심부로 거듭났고, 최근 공원이자 도시의 유산으로 탈바꿈하였다. 공원의 스포츠, 문화, 교육 그리고 환경은 새롭게 들어선 주변의 커뮤니티와 연결점을 제시하였다. 올림픽 경기 당시 중앙 광장으로 기능하던 넓은 포장 부지는, 오늘날 강과 운하 그리고 멋진 건축물—자하 하디드의 수영 경기장, 아니쉬 카푸어의 전망 타워인 아르셀로미탈 오빗 등—로 둘러싸인 22헥타르 이상의 공원이 되었다.

경관의 네 가지 틀

퀸 엘리자베스 올림픽 파크가 제공하는 프로그램들의 중심지인 사우스 파크는 네 가지 경관 틀로 이해할 수 있는데, 이는 부지를 체계적으로 조직할 뿐 아니라, 매우 친밀하고 사교적인 공간인 일련의 '플레저 가든'을 형성하는 틀로 작용한다.

'원호형 산책로'는 사우스 파크의 새로운 중추이자 주요한 사교적 장치. 이 산책로는 전체 공원의 남북을 대담하게 가로지르며, 공원의 주요 공간들과 명소들을 연결한다. 한가로이 거닐 수 있는 널찍한 산책로인 원호는 공원의 방문객들을 강력하게 유도하며 시각적으로 활짝 열린 시야를 제공한다. 정형적인 형태의 커다란 나무들이 열식된 산책로는 다양한 범위의 사교를 위한 가구를 제공하는 한편, 여러 가지 종류의 파빌리온, 키오스크, 그리고 선형 마켓, 축제, 장터 등 이벤트 공간의 장이 된다.

'식재 리본'은 5m 너비의 어린 나무, 관목, 그리고 키

77

큰 풀섶과 다년생 초화류 등으로 구성된 식재 띠다. 이는 원호형 산책로의 서쪽 경계를 극적인 형태로 구불구불 따라 올라가며, 사교 모임과 이벤트 프로그램을 위한 '외실'과 공간을 효과적으로 구획한다. 이들 공간으로 진입할 수 있는 식재 리본 사이의 열린 틈은 넉넉한 통행 공간과 부지 지하에 매설된 인프라스트럭처의 위치 등을 고려하여 세심하게 배치되었다.

'이벤트 외실'은 공연, 공공 예술, 이벤트 또는 볼거리 등을 제공하기 위해 가변적이고 융통성 있게 구성된 공간이다. 이벤트 외실들은 발주처에서 요구한 다양한 규모의 이벤트—대규모 콘서트와 축제부터 작은 그룹 모임, 전시, 공연 또는 연주회 등—를 수용할 수 있도록 매우 다양한 크기로 구성되었다.

공원의 서쪽과 남쪽에는 다양한 크기의 '잔디밭과 정원'들이 조성되어 있다. 이들은 공원의 동쪽에 위치한 동적 이용을 위한 포장된 공간과 상반되게, 가변적이고 수동적인 이용이 가능한 부드러운 녹지 공간이다.

이러한 경관의 틀은 일상적인 이용과 즐거움뿐만 아니라 다양한 종류의 이벤트 프로그램—식도락 축제, 장터, 대규모 콘서트부터 놀이용 탈것, 작은 규모의 서커스, 공연, 예술 전시, 문화 및 교육 프로그램에 이르기까지—을 아우를 수 있는 강력한 공간을 만들어 냈다.

식재

공원 디자인의 핵심인 식재 리본은 다양한 '생울타리'로 손쉽게 드나들 수 있는 열린 공간을 만드는가 하면, 빽빽하고 위요된 형태의 공간을 구성하기도 한다. 어느 지점에서는 질감이 느껴지는 풀숲과 꽃무더기로, 어떤 공간은 야생이 뒤섞인 형태로, 또 다른 곳에서는 덤불과 같은 형태로 나타난다. 다양한 수종으로 이루어진 변화무쌍한 형태의 생울타리는 공원 전체의 서식처를 향상시키며, 새와 나비뿐만 아니라 여타 동물의 생육을 돕는다.

원호형 산책로에는 큰 수목들이 2열로 식재되어, 나무와 나무 사이에 만들어진 캐노피가 산책로에 멋들어진 그늘을 제공한다. 이 수목들은 부지의 북쪽으로 가면서 점점 더 다양한 수종으로 변화하는데, 이는 공원 북쪽의 자유롭고 덜 형식적인 분위기를 반영한다. 화목류 수종들은 '잔디밭과 정원들'을 따라 흩뿌리듯 식재되어 있고, 공원 지하의 인프라스트럭처의 위치를 고려하여 위치를 선정하였다.

가구

사우스 파크의 가구는 이용객들의 넓고 다양한 범위의 사교적인 소통을 돕기 위하여 디자인하고 배치되었다. 일련의 넉넉한 크기의 가구들을 원호형 산책로를 따라서, 그리고 이벤트 외실 곳곳에, 중요 지점에 전략적으로 배치하여 공원을 더욱 더 친밀한 공간으로 만들었다. 공원에 이용된 가구들은 올림픽 게임 중에 사용된 기존 가구를 포함하며, 목재, 금속재, 그리고 콘크리트를 사용한 새로운 가구들이 보완되었다. 가구의 재료는 디자인의 의도를 더욱 강화시킬 수 있고, 시간이 지나 공원이 성장함에 따라 유동적으로 대처할 수 있는 재료를 기준으로 선정하였다. 이렇게 선정된 재료들은 내구성이 있고, 재활용이 가능하며, 지속가능하다.

The Play Room is a major draw for the Park, attracting children and families because of its mix of play and risk. The design supports not only climbing but also hiding, swinging, crawling, and jumping.

Theatre Room

놀이

공원은 사교 모임과 재미있는 공공의 참여를 가능한 많이 유도하는 방향으로 설계되었다. '분수 미로'는 식재 리본의 형태를 본떠 만든 선형 수경 시설로 선형이 감싸는 공간에 일련의 '외실'을 만들어 낸다. 분수 미로는 1.5m 너비의 턱이 없는 콘크리트 포장 띠로, 분수 노즐이 띠의 중앙을 따라 규칙적으로 배치되어 있다. 각각의 분수는 저전압 수중 펌프를 사용하여, 개별의 분수를 컨트롤할 수 있게 하였다. 이러한 환상적인 컨트롤은 이용자가 물과 상호 교감하고 즐길 수 있도록 해 주었다. 분수를 지원하는 기계 설비실과 물탱크는 기존의 건물 기초 아래에 위치하여 올림픽 경기 시 이용하던 계단과 연결 통로를 통하여 접근할 수 있게 하였다.

'놀이 시설'은 원호형 산책로를 따라 위치하고 있다. 이 시설들은 목재로 만든 현관용 그네, 오르내릴 수 있는 '주판형' 사다리, 그리고 앉아서 편히 쉴 수 있는 시설과 공간을 포함한다. 공원의 동쪽 경계인 원호형 산책로를 따라, 나무 그늘 아래에서 다른 벤치나 건물들과 연계할 수 있도록 이 시설들을 배치하였으며, 놀이 시설은 일정하게 정해진 이용 방식 없이 다양한 방식으로 전 연령이 손쉽게 접근하여 이용할 수 있도록 제안되었다.

'놀이 외실'은 이벤트 외실 안에 위치한 방 안의 방이다. 극적인 효과를 위하여 붉은 색으로 테마를 정했고(붉은 색 아크릴 코팅을 한 아스팔트와 붉은색 고무칩 놀이 바닥재 포장을 포함하여), 이용자와 상호 소통할 수 있는 놀이 시설들을 배치하였다. 놀이 시설은 대형 바위, 맞춤 제작된 오름 벽, 워터 펌프, 그리고 다양한 목재 놀이 시설 등으로 구성되어 있다. 시설의 디자인은 오르기, 숨기, 그네타기, 기어 다니기, 그리고 뛰어 오르기 등의 다양한 활동을 가능하도록 해준다. 이 놀이 외실의 포장은 모든 연령대의 어린이들과 가족들 모두가 놀이할 수 있는 다양한 공간을 제공하기 위하여 고무, 모래, 잔디 등을 섞어 사용하였다. 아이들이 뛰어 노는 동안 부모들은 근처의 잔디밭이나 산책로 가에 위치한 그늘 아래 벤치에 앉아 쉴 수 있다.

사우스 파크는 동 런던의 방치된 공간이었던 이 장소의 사회적, 경제적, 환경적인 변화를 이끌어내는 촉매제로 작용하고 있을 뿐만 아니라, 로어 리 밸리 지역을 재활성화하는 데에도 기여하고 있다. 퀸 엘리자베스 올림픽 파크의 북쪽 공원 부지가 평화롭고, 아름답고, 멋진 경치의 '천천히 움직이는' 경관으로 남아 있는 반면, 사우스 파크는 더 많은 움직임과 볼거리, 방문객과의 상호 작용과 다양한 이벤트를 촉진시키고 있다. **번역** 안동혁

James Corner Field Operations
The 3rd Section of the High Line

Design James Corner Field Operations (Project Lead), Diller Scofidio + Renfro and Piet Oudolf
Design Consultants Buro Happold, Robert Silman Associates, L'Observatoire International, Pentagram Design, Inc., Site Masters Inc., Northern Designs, Roux Associates, Inc., Philip Habib & Associates, Inc., MKJ Communications
Construction Manager Sciame(Landscape Design), Liro(Site Preparation)
Construction Subconsultants BPDL, CAC, Concrete Industries One, Steven Dubner Landscaping, Egg, L&L Painting, Sunny Border, Venture, FMB, Sawkill Lumber, Site Works, ATTA Inc., Landscape Structures, Sturio dell'Arte, Optical Mechanics Inc., VGS
Client The City of New York, Friends of the High Line
Location West Side of Manhattan, New York, NY, USA
Section 1 Gansevoort Street to 20th Street
Section 2 20th Street to 30th Street
Section 3 West Side Rail Yards: 30th to 34th Street
Planning 2006~present
Completion In Progress(3rd section opened on 2014. 9. 21.)
Photographs James Corner Field Operations and Diller Scofidio + Renfro, Courtesy of the City of New York, Iwan Bann

The High Line is a public park built on a historic freight rail line elevated above the streets on Manhattan's west side. It is owned by the City of New York, and maintained and operated by Friends of the High Line. Founded in 1999 by community residents, Friends of the High Line fought for the High Line's preservation and transformation at a time when the historic structure was under the threat of demolition. It is now the non-profit conservancy working with the New York City Department of Parks & Recreation to make sure the High Line is maintained as an extraordinary public space for all visitors to enjoy. In addition to overseeing maintenance, operations, and public programming for the park, Friends of the High Line works to raise the essential private funds to support virtually all of the park's annual operating budget, and to advocate for the preservation and transformation of the High Line at the Rail Yards, the third and final section of the historic structure, which runs between West 30th and West 34th Streets.

High Line

Inspired by the melancholic, "found" beauty of the High Line, where nature has reclaimed a once-vital piece of urban infrastructure, the design aims to re-fit this industrial conveyance into a post-industrial instrument of leisure. By changing the rules of engagement between plant life and pedestrians, our strategy of "agri-tecture" combines organic and building materials into a blend of changing proportions that accommodates the wild, the cultivated, the intimate, and the social. In stark contrast to the speed of Hudson River Park, the singular linear experience of the new High Line landscape is marked by slowness, distraction and other-worldliness that preserves the strange, wild character of the High Line, yet doesn't underestimate its intended use and popularity as a new public space. This notion underpins the overall strategy—the invention of a new paving and planting system that allows for varying ratios of hard to soft surface that transition from high use areas(100% hard) to richly vegetated biotopes(100% soft), with a variety of experiential gradients in between.

HIGH LINE SECTION 1
GANSEVOORT STREET TO WEST 20TH STREET

HIGH LINE SECTION 2
WEST 20TH STREET TO WEST 30TH STREET

HIGH LINE AT THE RAIL YARDS
WEST 30TH STREET TO WEST 34TH STREET

High Line key plan

Aerial view of Section 3 of the High Line
along 30th Street

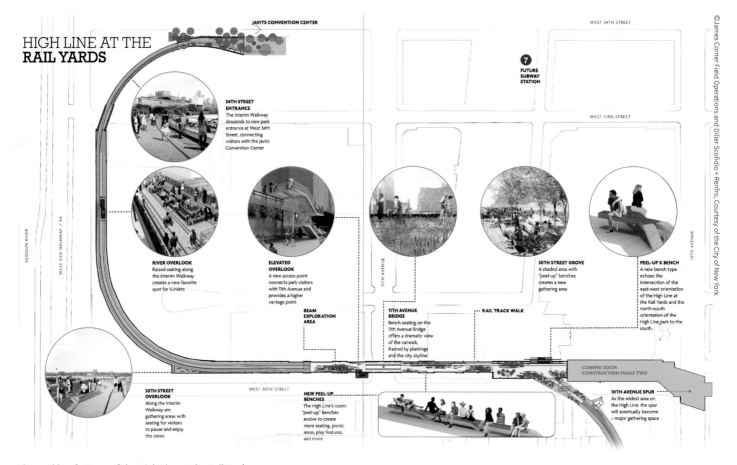

HIGH LINE AT THE RAIL YARDS

JAVITS CONVENTION CENTER

WEST 34TH STREET

WEST 33RD STREET

7 FUTURE SUBWAY STATION

34TH STREET ENTRANCE
The Interim Walkway descends to new park entrance at West 34th Street, connecting visitors with the Javits Convention Center

RIVER OVERLOOK
Raised seating along the Interim Walkway creates a new favorite spot for sunsets

ELEVATED OVERLOOK
A new access point connects park visitors with 11th Avenue and provides a higher vantage point

BEAM EXPLORATION AREA

30TH STREET GROVE
A shaded area with "peel-up" benches creates a new gathering area

PEEL-UP X BENCH
A new bench type echoes the intersection of the east-west orientation of the High Line at the Rail Yards and the north-south orientation of the High Line park to the south.

11TH AVENUE BRIDGE
Bench seating on the 11th Avenue Bridge offers a dramatic view of the catwalk, framed by plantings and the city skyline

RAIL TRACK WALK

COMING SOON CONSTRUCTION PHASE TWO

30TH STREET OVERLOOK
Along the Interim Walkway are gathering areas with seating for visitors to pause and enjoy the views

WEST 30TH STREET

NEW PEEL-UP BENCHES
The High Line's iconic "peel-up" benches evolve to create more seating, picnic areas, play features, and more

10TH AVENUE SPUR
As the widest area on the High Line, the spur will eventually become a major gathering space

HUDSON RIVER · WEST SIDE HIGHWAY / 9A · 11TH AVENUE · 10TH AVENUE

Plan and key features of the High Line at the Rail Yards

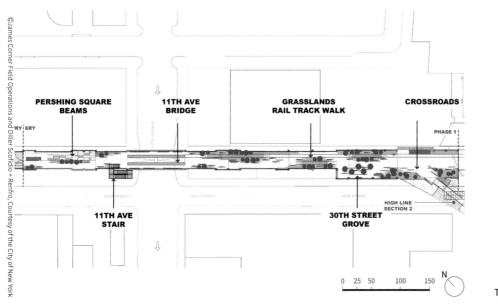

PERSHING SQUARE BEAMS

11TH AVE BRIDGE

GRASSLANDS RAIL TRACK WALK

CROSSROADS

PHASE 1

11TH AVE STAIR

30TH STREET GROVE

HIGH LINE SECTION 2

0 25 50   100   150   **N**

The Eastern Rail Yards

The Rail Track Walks expose the High Line's rail tracks.

The design approach respects the character of the High Line itself: its singularity and linearity, its straight-forward pragmatism, its emergent properties with wild plant-life—meadows, thickets, vines, mosses, flowers—intermixed with ballast, steel and concrete. Our solution is primarily threefold: first the paving system, built from linear concrete planks with open joints, specially tapered edges and seams that permit intermingling of plant-life with harder materials. Less a pathway and more a combed or furrowed landscape, this intermixing creates a textural effect of immersion, strolling "within" rather than feeling distanced from. The selection and arrangement of grasses and plants further helps to define a wild, dynamic character, distinct from a typical manicured landscape, and representative of the extreme conditions and shallow rooting depth. The second strategy is to slow things down, to promote a sense of duration and of being in another place, where time seems less pressing. Long stairways, meandering pathways, and hidden niches encourage taking one's time. The third approach involved a careful sense of dimension of scale, minimizing the current tendency to make things bigger and obvious and seeking instead a more subtle gauge of the High Line's measure. The result is an episodic and varied sequence of public spaces and landscapes set along a simple and consistent line—a line that cuts across some of the most remarkable elevated vistas of Manhattan and the Hudson River.

High Line Section 3

Representing one-third of the entire High Line, Section 3 is one of the most iconic stretches of the High Line with expansive views of the Hudson River and the Midtown skyline. Here, we were challenged to continue to build upon the identity and success of the existing High Line, yet find a different way to respond to the radically new, 21st-century context of the Hudson Yards development. The design takes advantage of the east-west orientation to the river, respects the existing wild landscape and industrial aesthetic, and introduces the next iteration of design elements. This latter section along the Western Rail Yards and 12th Avenue is perhaps the most authentically subtle design, where the "original" High Line landscape, with its self-sown grasses and flowers emerging from old tracks, wood ties and stone ballast, remains intact.

Peel-up Benches

Expanding the vocabulary of the iconic High Line "peel-up" bench, new types of benches have been introduced on Section 3 to create a more social environment including the peel-up picnic, peel-up conversation bench with facing backs, peel-up long bench—an extra long bench that encourages interaction of large groups, the peel-up sound bench—a chime feature for children and the peel-up rocker and interactive bench that responds to how people sit and move.

Evoking the High Line's history as an active freight rail line, the Rail Track Walks incorporate with artifacts such as the rail "frog."

©Iwan Baan

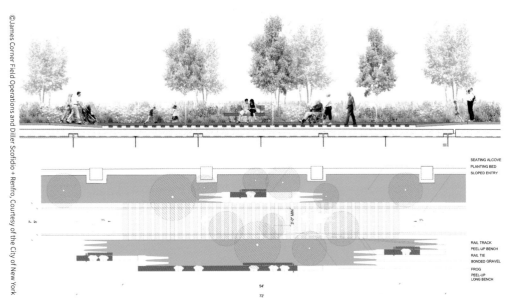

SEATING ALCOVE
PLANTING BED
SLOPED ENTRY

RAIL TRACK
PEEL-UP BENCH
RAIL TIE
BONDED GRAVEL
FROG
PEEL-UP
LONG BENCH

54'

72'

Typical plan and section of the Rail Track Walk

Typical Rail Track Walk paving details

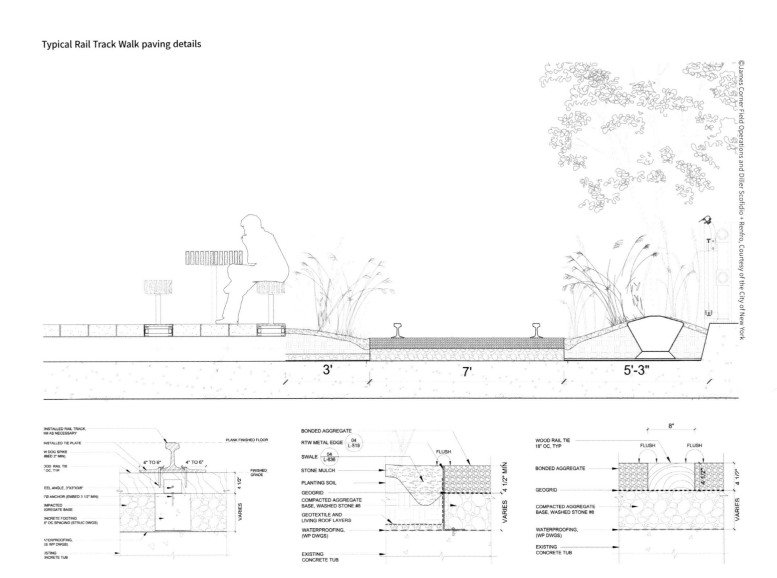

3'   7'   5'-3"

INSTALLED RAIL TRACK,
RIM AS NECESSARY

INSTALLED TIE PLATE

PLANK FINISHED FLOOR

W DOG SPIKE
(BED 2" MIN)

4" TO 6"   4" TO 6"

FINISHED GRADE

OOD RAIL TIE
" OC, TYP

4 1/2"

EEL ANGLE, 3"X3"X3/8"

"Ø ANCHOR (EMBED 3 1/2" MIN)

MPACTED
GGREGATE BASE

VARIES

CONCRETE FOOTING
6" OC SPACING (STRUC DWGS)

ATERPROOFING,
EE WP DWGS)

ISTING
ONCRETE TUB

BONDED AGGREGATE

RTW METAL EDGE   04 / L-519

SWALE   04 / L-636

STONE MULCH

PLANTING SOIL

GEOGRID

COMPACTED AGGREGATE
BASE, WASHED STONE #8

GEOTEXTILE AND
LIVING ROOF LAYERS

WATERPROOFING,
(WP DWGS)

EXISTING
CONCRETE TUB

FLUSH

4 1/2" MIN   VARIES

WOOD RAIL TIE
18" OC, TYP

8"

FLUSH   FLUSH

BONDED AGGREGATE

GEOGRID

COMPACTED AGGREGATE
BASE, WASHED STONE #8

WATERPROOFING,
(WP DWGS)

EXISTING
CONCRETE TUB

4 1/2"   4 1/2"   VARIES

The Rail Track Walk

Crossroads

The Crossroads marks the intersection where the north-south sections of the High Line meet the east-west section running along 30th Street. Here, the visitor has a choice—they can walk south along the High Line all the way to Gansevoort; they can walk west to the Hudson River and in the future, they can walk north onto the new Hudson Yards plaza and Culture Shed and on to the Hudson Boulevard; or they can walk east through the large new "passage" to the High Line Spur across Tenth Avenue. The Crossroads is therefore a point of choice, a point of arrival and a point of departure. It is a meeting place, a point of juncture, where people come together, re-orient and disperse. To signify the importance of this location, we kept the design simple and open. The characteristic planks of the paving take a turn from running north-south to east-west through a series of special "X" and "Y" plank forms. A special "X-bench" marks the center.

30th Street Grove

The 30th Street Grove is a serene space defined by a social grouping of benches or "flocks" under the canopy of Kentucky Coffee Trees. The "flock" arrangements allow a porosity and non-hierarchical movement while encouraging social interaction between park users.

Rail Track Walk

Three linear walks expose the High Line's rail tracks, evoking the High Line's history as an active freight rail line and allowing the users to experience the tracks in a new way. On the Rail Track Walks, visitors can interact with original artifacts such as the rail "frog" and the rail switches, or rest in one of several seating alcoves located throughout the pathways. The pathway is constructed of bonded aggregate with wooden ties in a flush condition surrounded by naturalistic planting beds.

88

The 30th Street Grove, a serene gathering space under the canopy of Kentucky Coffee Trees, houses an assortment of new design elements, including the peel-up sound bench and the peel-up rocker.

New Peel-up Furniture typologies

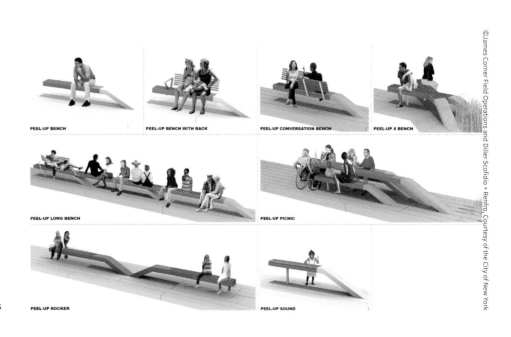

PEEL-UP BENCH

PEEL-UP BENCH WITH BACK

PEEL-UP CONVERSATION BENCH

PEEL-UP X BENCH

PEEL-UP LONG BENCH

PEEL-UP PICNIC

PEEL-UP ROCKER

PEEL-UP SOUND

11th Avenue Bridge

As the High Line runs west over 11th Avenue, the main pathway gradually slopes up about two feet, creating an elevated catwalk from which visitors can view the park, the cityscape, and Hudson River. Lush display gardens on either side of the catwalk separate the main pathway from the more intimate linear bench seating running along the railing on either side of the bridge.

Pershing Square Beams

Just west of 11th Avenue is a unique design feature for kids, the Pershing Square Beams. Here the High Line's concrete deck is stripped away, revealing the original framework of steel beams and girders. The structure itself is transformed into a series of sunken areas—coated in a silicone surface for safety—that children can run between, climb over, and play within.

A series of interactive play elements have been developed that are unique to the High Line. These include a rotating beam, three periscopes, a gopher hole and three talk/view tubes. The painted vertical surfaces of the beams incorporate a stenciled naming system extracted from the original 1930's Construction Documents.

Interim Walkway

The Interim Walkway, built over the existing, self-seeded landscape at the Western Rail Yards, was constructed to make this section of the High Line accessible and safe for the public as soon as possible and to complete the experience of walking along the entire length of the High Line, from one end to the other.

The path is situated between a set of the existing rail tracks and includes the 12th Avenue Overlook, River Overlook and entry plaza at 34th Street, where the existing High Line ramps down to grade. At the 12th Avenue Overlook, an existing High Line beam, cut from the structure has been retrofitted into a large-scale seating platform. A second version of this element is incorporated at the 34th Street entry plaza. The River Overlook, composed of stacked reclaimed Douglas Fir timbers, provides a gathering space for visitors to enjoy expansive views of the Hudson River to the west and an usual panorama of the Rail Yards to the east.

Section of the 11th Avenue Bridge

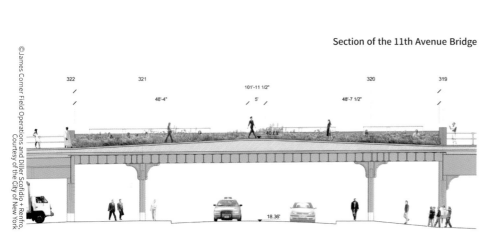

As the High Line runs west over 11th Avenue, the main pathway gradually slopes up two feet, creating an elevated catwalk from which visitors can view the and Hudson River.

©Iwan Bann

하이라인은 맨해튼의 웨스트사이드에 건설된 고가 폐선 철로 위에 조성된 공원이다. 1999년 설립된 비영리 단체 하이라인 친구들은 현재 뉴욕 공원관리국은 물론 지역 주민과의 긴밀한 협의를 통해 보다 나은 하이라인을 만들기 위해 많은 노력을 기울이고 있다. 이런 노력이 제임스 코너 필드 오퍼레이션스의 설계안으로 이어졌다.

하이라인의 설계 전략

한때 도시의 중추적 기능을 담당했던 도시 기반 시설의 일부가 자연 발생적으로 자라난 야생 식물로 뒤덮였다. 산업 유산을 도시 휴양 공간으로 탈바꿈하려는 목적을 달성하기 위한 하이라인의 설계 전략은 방치되었던 공간에서 (예상치 못하게) '발견된' 아름다움에서 착안된다. 식생과 보행자들의 관계를 재설정하는 과정을 나타내는, 이른바 'agri–tecture' 전략은 생물과 건축 재료를 결합하여 야생과 경작된 자연, 개인적이면서도 사회적인 공간이 공존하는 장소를 만들어낸다. 이렇게 만들어진 하이라인의 단일한 선형 공간은 느리면서도 오락적인, 그리고 주변과는 다른 비현실적인 모습을 담고 있으며 인근의 허드슨 리버 파크가 만들어내는 속도감 있는 경관과는 극명한 차이를 보인다. 하이라인은 기존 여타 공원에 비해 낯설고 거친 야생의 모습을 그대로 경험하도록 유도하지만 그런 방식의 경험이 새롭게 조성된 공공 공간의 의도된 디자인 요소나 대중적인 가치를 떨어뜨리지 않는다.

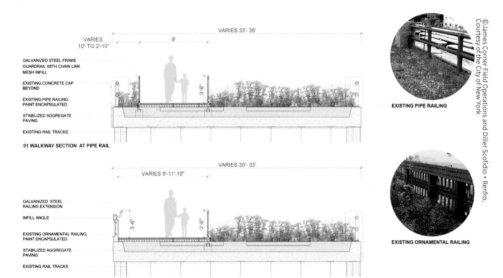

Typical WRY interim walkway sections

Situated in between a set of the existing rail tracks, the Western Rail Yards temporary walkway allows visitors to experience the existing, self-seeded landscape.

©Iwan Bann

The Western Rail Yards interim walkway offers visitors expansive views of the Hudson River.

하이라인의 설계안은 이 폐선 부지만의 고유한 특성을 존중한다. 하이라인만의 특이성과 선형성, 직설적 실용주의, 초지와 잡목 숲, 덩굴 식물, 이끼류, 그리고 야생화에서 볼 수 있는 식물의 창발적인 특성이 철로와 자갈 바닥, 콘크리트와 같은 인공적 소재와 섞여있는 모습을 보존 및 특화하는 전략을 내세우는 것이다. 이 전략은 크게 세 가지로 구성된다.

첫 번째 전략은 하이라인만의 바닥 포장 시스템이다. 열린 이음의 선형 콘크리트 판은 특히 테이퍼드 에지를 통해 식물과 자연스럽게 섞여 들어가는 시스템을 구현한다. 하이라인 위의 그라스와 식물은 대상지의 얕은 식재 기반과 같이 좋지 않은 생육 환경에서도 살아님을 수 있다. 이곳의 야생 식물은 일반적인 공원에서 볼 수 있는 깔끔하게 정리되어 식재된 모습과는 달리 역동적인 분위기를 만들어낸다. 두 번째 전략은 이러한 전혀 새로운 세계 속에 있는 듯한 체험의 지속 시간을 연장시키는 것이다. 긴 계단과 구불구불한 길들, 그리고 숨겨진 벽감들은 사람들이 하이라인을 충분히 느끼고 경험할 수 있는 시간을 갖도록 한다. 세 번째 전략은 공간감의 세심한 조정을 통한 접근법을 취한다. 기존 공원이 보여주는 크고, 눈에 띄는 공간감을 최소화하는 대신, 하이라인의 조건에서만 가능한 미묘한 공간감을 담아내려는 것이다.

하이라인 3구역

3구역은 하이라인 전체 구역 중 가장 상징적인 공간으로 허드슨 리버와 미드타운의 스카이라인을 담아내는 화려한 조망을 제공한다. 3구역의 설계에서 중점을 둔 사항은 하이라인이라는 프로젝트의 정체성과 1, 2구역의 리노베이션 성과를 이어나가는 것에 그치지 않고 2015년 완공된 허드슨 야드의 급진적인 21세기형 개발에 대응할 수 있는 방법을 제시하는 것이다. 3구역의 설계안은 강에 대한 동서양 문화권의 견해를 담아내며 현존하는 야생과 산업 유산의 미학적 가치를 존중하고, 하이라인의 상징적인 디자인 요소들을 1, 2구역과는 다른 형태로 새롭게 제시한다.

하이라인의 주요 디자인 요소 중에 하나인 필-업 벤치는 그 이름이 나타내는 것처럼 지반을 깎아 올린 형태의 벤치로 다양한 모임이 가능한 사회적 공간이다. 3구역에는 1, 2구역에서는 볼 수 없던 새로운 형태와 기능의 필-업 벤치가 도입되었다. 필-업 사운드 벤치는 필-업 벤치에 실로폰이 결합된 것으로 청각적 즐거움을 제공하고, 필-업 로커는 시소의 기능이 적용되어 사람들의 움직임에 자연스럽게 반응한다. 필-업 피크닉 벤치와 필-업 롱 벤치는 한 번에 많은 사람이 앉을 수 있게 디자인되었고, 필-업 대화형 벤치는 서로 마주볼 수 있는 벤치라는 아주 간단하지만 신선한 형태를 취한다. 이런 각양각색의 필-업 벤치들은 30번가 그로브 구간 곳곳에 배치되어 공원을 이용하는 다양한 사람들이 자연스럽게 교류할 수 있는 사교적인 분위기를 만들어 낸다.

일련의 기찻길과 나무 수풀로 이루어진 보행로인 레일 트랙 워크는 사람들로 하여금 걷고 싶은 분위기를 만들어 낸다. 보행로를 따라 곳곳에 숨겨진 벤치에서 휴식을 취할 수도 있다. 노출된 철로와 더불어 철로 교차점에 설치된 철차와 선로 변환기 등의 디테일은 하이라인 3구역의 과거를 상상해볼 수 있게 한다.

11번가를 가로지르는 부분의 공중보행로는 고가로부터 약 2피트 정도의 높이 차이를 가진 경사면의 형태를 보인다. 이렇게 주변보다 높은 위치에 있는 11번가 브리지는 하이라인, 도시 경관, 그리고 허드슨 리버를 향해 새로운 시야를 경험하게 한다. 이 공중보행로 양쪽에 우거진 정원은 공중보행로를 난간을 따라 배치된 벤치들과 분리시켜 보조보행로를 보다 사적인 공간으로 만들어준다.

11번가 브리지를 지나면 아이들을 위한 놀이 공간으로 설계된 퍼싱 스퀘어 빔즈를 만나볼 수 있다. 하이라인의 콘크리트를 걷어내고 철제 빔과 대들보로 이루어진 골격을 그대로 드러내었고 이 골격은 안전을 위해 실리콘으로 코팅되었다. 이렇게 선큰된 공간은 뛰어다니고, 기어오르며, 장난치고 놀 수 있는 독특한 놀이 경관를 만들어 낸다. 퍼싱 스퀘어 빔즈는 아이들을 위한 공간으로 회전하는 빔이나 잠망경과 같은 놀이 기구도 설치되며, 철골

The interim walkway currently features
a site-specific High Line Art commission
by Adrián Villar Rojas

© Iwan Baan

The River Overlook, composed of stacked reclaimed timbers, provides a gathering space for visitors to enjoy expansive views of the Hudson River to the west.

River Overlook construction details

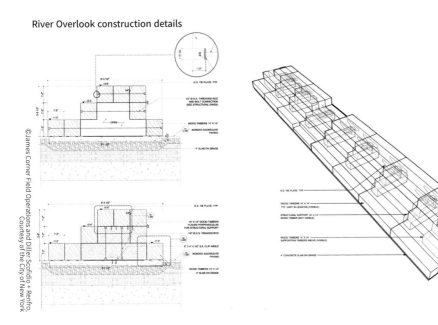

© James Corner Field Operations and Diller Scofidio + Renfro, Courtesy of the City of New York

구조를 둘러싸고 조성될 감각 정원은 다양한 향과 질감의 꽃들로 아이들에게 발견과 탐험의 욕구를 불러일으킬 것이다.

웨스턴 레일 야드에 조성된 임시 구간은 허드슨 리버의 모습을 더욱 극적으로 바라볼 수 있는 12번가 전망대와 강변 전망대, 그리고 웨스트 34번가로 이어지는 입구 광장을 포함한다.

3구역에서는 하이라인 프로그램의 하나인 하이라인 공공 예술 프로젝트의 일환으로 설치된 로하스의 예술 작품도 확인 할 수 있다. 2004년부터 시작된 하이라인 프로젝트의 마침표를 찍는 하이라인 3구역은 기존의 웨스턴 레일 야드와 12번가 사이의 도시 배경과 자연이 키워낸 그라스와 야생화들이 오래된 철길과, 나무 침목, 자갈 바닥과 같은 산업 유산과 가장 절묘하게 디자인된 결과물일 것이다. **번역** 양다빈

James Corner Field Operations

Tongva Park

Landscape Architect James Corner Field Operations(James Corner, Lisa Tziona Switkin, Sarah Weidner Astheimer, Matt Grunbaum, David Christensen, Tsutomu Bessho, Yitian Wang)
Contractor W. E. O'Neil
Architecture for Restroom Frederick Fisher & Partners
Structural & MEP Engineering BuroHappold
Civil Engineering Fuscoe Engineering
Lighting Design HLB
Water Feature Design Fluidity Design Consultants
Horticulture Perry & Associates, Greenlee & Associates
Irrigation d.d. Pagano, Inc.
Urban Soils Wallace Labs
Geotechnical Engineer Converse Consultants
Artist Iñigo Manglano-Ovalle
Client·Owner The City of Santa Monica
Location Santa Monica, California, USA
Area 7.2ac
Completion 2013
Photographs James Corner Field Operations, Jonathan Alcorn, Tim Street-Porter, Joakim Lloyd Raboff, Angie Smith

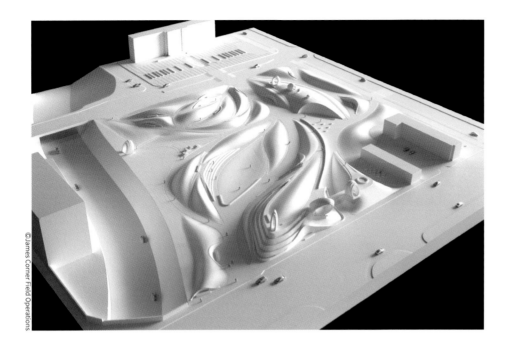

Tongva Park + Ken Genser Square embody a new type of urban landscape that is active, innovative, resource-conscious, and natural. Shaped by extensive public participation, the design creates a contemporary and transformative series of gardens and active spaces that symbolically redefine and interconnect the center of Santa Monica.

Concept model. An early topographic model of the park reveals a sculpted landscape of dramatically rising and falling hills, which are inspired by washes and ravines that once occupied the site.

Observation Hill
1. Ocean Ave Shaded Seating Green Screen
2. Ocean Ave Water Feature
3. Grand Bluff
4. Pier Overlook
5. Ocean Overlook
6. Public Restroom

Gathering Hill
7. Amphitheater + Lawn
8. Fig Picnic Grove

Discovery Hill
9. Tree Grove + Seating
10. Discovery Play Area
11. Hilltop Play Forts
12. The Village Gateway

Garden Hill
13. Water Bay
14. Gardens

Ken Genser Square
15. Water Feature
16. Lawn Areas

Situated between City Hall and Ocean Avenue, park paths aspire to reach beyond the project boundary. They connect the civic campus with Santa Monica's active urban core and views of the city's defining landscape features beyond: the ocean and mountains.

©Tim Street-Porter

Seating terraces shaded by Strawberry trees compose Gathering Hill,
which is the social and civic heart of the park. The seating terraces function well for casual gatherings
as well as formal events such as Santa Monica's "Jazz on the Lawn."

Project Overview

Situated on 7.4 acres between City Hall, the I-10 freeway, and Santa Monica's iconic palm tree
lined Ocean Avenue, Tongva Park + Ken Genser Square have transformed a derelict and flat
parking lot into lush landscape of rolling hills, swales, mediterranean meadow gardens, and
active urban spaces.

Inspired by the Southern California arroyo landscape of washes and ravines that once defined
the site, a series of braided pathways appear to organically emerge from the footsteps of City
Hall, extend west, and weave the park into the fabric of the city. Dramatic rising and falling
topography reinforces the fluid pathway system and organize the site into four thematic hilltop
areas, each calibrated to a different primary use and experience.

Garden Hill is defined by a series of seating alcoves and intimate display gardens that showcase
a mix of seasonally dynamic, native, and appropriately adapted Southern California plants.

Discovery Hill is a play space for children, offering a range of discovery experiences with hill
slides, a music wall, water play, and forts embedded into a lush and shaded landscape.

Observation Hill reaches a height of 18 feet, and offers the best views of the ocean and
neighboring vicinity, including overlooks, a bridge, and a remarkably bright and airy public
restroom tucked under the hill.

Gathering Hill provides open space for congregation and relaxation and includes a large multipurpose lawn, shaded seating terraces, and an informal picnic area.

Ken Genser Square provides new space for civic gathering and complements the City Hall
landmark building with its symmetrical footprint, low pre-cast seat walls, and gently rolling
grassy hills.

Planting

The most dramatic aspect of the site transformation is its ecological restoration. Over three hundred carefully selected new trees, thousands of new plants, and hundreds of different California native and appropriately adapted species are part of the project's abundant and ambitious planting scheme. Tongva Park and Ken Genser Square are one of the first large scale contemporary urban projects to highlight California native plants as significant horticultural features and offer the largest-scale mediterranean meadow garden of its complexity in a public space.

Existing trees were preserved and form an important backbone for new plant material. "Morty," a large Moreton bay fig tree, fondly named by Santa Monica residents hosts a picnic grove near its impressive canopy. "The Three Amigos," three mature Ficus trees, were successfully relocated close by to create a "Fig Grove" that dramatically buffers the freeway, while existing palms are clustered close to the park's main entry to provide vertical structure along the park's edge. New trees are grouped into three forest types, which are modeled on native California coastal scrub, chaparral, and riparian plant communities. They are carefully positioned to take advantage of the site's numerous microclimates, provide the framework for the project's extensive plant palette, and contribute to the distinctiveness of spaces within the park. Discovery Hill hosts more trees than any other part of the park. It combines silvery olives and oaks for maximum shade. Groves of pines can be found nearby at Observation Hill. Its terraced western edge faces south to some of the toughest site conditions and features Blond ambition grass interlaced with cascading succulents, aloes, and agave. Western sycamores weave their way between the hills at swales and low points to frame a soft meadow interior that features grasses, wild flowers, and mediterranean bulbs. Appropriately adapted specimen trees selected for their flower or distinctive form increase the diversity of species within the park and are located within Garden Hill and along the park's central path.

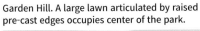
Garden Hill. A large lawn articulated by raised pre-cast edges occupies center of the park.

©Tim Street-Porter

Overlooks fabricated from plasma cut plate steel create a contemporary and striking park edge. They are as much about outward view as windows into the park, enticing passersby to enter the site.

Observation Hill and Ocean Avenue Gateway. The primary entrance into the park at Ocean Avenue is defined by a lengthy water feature, which engages the side of Observation Hill. Planted terraces topped by a stand of Stone Pines also define this striking entry.

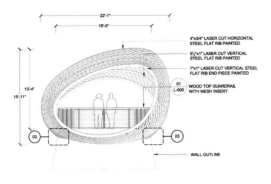

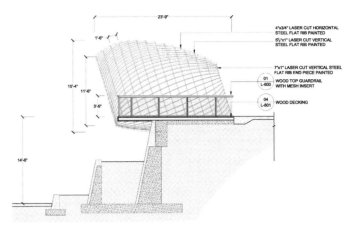

Overlook 1 - Front elevation   Overlook 1 - Section

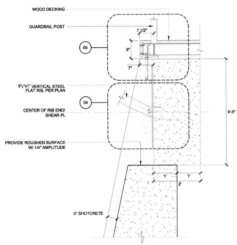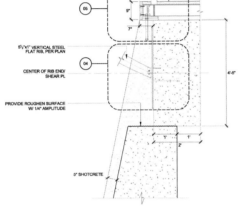

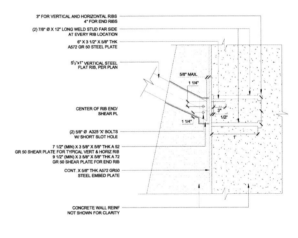

Steel anchor to concrete wall - Detail 1   Steel anchor to concrete wall - Detail 2

Architectural Features + Hardscape

Architectural features and a texturally rich hardscape palette of boulders and pebbles work with the park's lush meadow gardens to reinforce the site's "arroyo wash" history, while at the same time, create an exciting new visual identity for the project that is unique to Santa Monica.

Walls + Paths are formed from golden hued cast-in-place concrete that exposes locally sourced tumbled aggregates of varying sizes and scales. Large boulders compose walls and punctuate path edges to emphasize a relaxed informality.

Shell-like Overlooks are perched on top of the tallest of the park's hills to frame iconic views and vistas of Santa Monica and the ocean. They are fabricated from plasma cut plate steel with cutting patterns extracted directly from the Landscape Architect's 3D model and finished in a silvery white to complement the rich golden hues of the park's paths, walls, and meadow gardens.

Alcoves are carved into planted hillsides to create interior garden bays with seating for contemplation or exterior bays with bike racks and social seating for community comings and goings.

Water Elements are poetically linked by a single runnel that flows downhill to the ocean. Their volume and presence increases the closer they are to the main entry.

Layers of lighting rest lightly upon the site and are revealed as one ascends to the hilltops. As dusk turns to night the sculptural forms and woven pathways of Tongva Park and Ken Genser Square welcome visitors in a soft, warm light that responds to the three-dimensionality of the site. Shielded highly-efficient LED and HID luminaries have been placed throughout the Park and Square.

Ocean Overlook at Sunset. The Ocean Overlook was carefully situated to frame the best view of the Pacific Ocean from the site. It offers an intimate, partially enclosed setting, popular at sunset.

Surrounded by large boulders, a play area at Discovery Hill is the most popular space for children within the park.

©James Corner Field Operations

통바 파크 + 켄 겐서 광장은 새로운 유형의 도시 경관을 구현하고 있다. 이는 자원에 대한 인식을 바탕으로 하는 한편, 자연 친화적 성격을 띠고 있다. 광범위한 대중의 참여를 바탕으로 한 디자인은 현대적이고 변화무쌍한 일련의 정원 및 활동 공간을 창조하였다. 이 공간들은 산타모니카 중심부를 상징적으로 새롭게 정의하는 한편 도시와 상호 연결된 공원을 만들어준다.

통바 파크 + 켄 겐서 광장은 약 7.4에이커(약 30,000㎡) 부지에 자리 잡고 있으며, 시청사, I-10 고속도로, 그리고 산타모니카의 상징이라 할 수 있는 야자수가 늘어선 오션 애비뉴 사이에 위치한다. 이 공원은 버려진 채 무미건조한 모습만을 드러내던 주차장을 구불구불한 언덕, 풀이 무성한 습지, 지중해풍의 초지 공원, 그리고 활발한 도심 속 활동 공간 등으로 이루어진 울창한 경관으로 변모시켰다.

한때 이 지역을 특징짓던 남부 캘리포니아 지방 특유의 구불구불한 소협곡 경관에서 영감을 받아 여러 갈래로 뻗어나가는 일련의 오솔길을 디자인했다. 이 오솔길은 시청사 정문으로부터 유기적인 모습으로 등장해 서쪽으로 이어지고, 나아가 공원이 자연스럽게 도시 전체 망에 엮여 들어가도록 한다. 극적인 변화가 있는 지형 덕분에 부드러운 오솔길 구조가 한층 강화될 뿐만 아니라 각기 다른 테마를 바탕으로 한 네 곳의 언덕 지역이 유기적으로 연계될 수 있다. 이들 지역은 서로 다른 용도 및 사용자 경험을 바탕으로 설계되었다.

정원의 언덕은 일련의 좌석을 배치한 알코브와 친근한 성격의 감상 정원으로 구성했는데, 계절에 따라 역동적으로 변화하는 자생종 또는 토착화된 남부 캘리포니아의 식물들을 식재했다.

발견의 언덕은 어린이를 위한 놀이 공간으로, 언덕 미끄럼틀, 음악의 벽, 물놀이 시설, 그리고 놀이 요새 등 울창하고 그늘진 경관 속에 배치된 다채로운 모험 시설물들을 제공한다.

관찰의 언덕은 높이가 18피트에 이르며, 바닷가 및 인근 지역을 최상의 조건에서 조망할 수 있다. 전망대, 다리 등으로 구성되어 있으며, 밝고 경쾌한 공중 화장실이 언덕 아래에 숨겨져 있다.

만남의 언덕은 모임과 휴식을 위한 공공 공간을 제공하며, 대규모 다목적 잔디밭, 그늘진 좌석 테라스, 그리고 편안한 소풍 공간 등으로 구성되어 있다.

켄 겐서 광장은 시민들이 자유롭게 모일 수 있는 공간을 제공하는 한편, 대칭적인 모습과 구불구불한 잔디 언덕 등을 통해 랜드마크인 시청사 건물을 보완하는 역할을 한다.

식재

대상지의 변화로 나타나는 가장 도드라진 특징은 생태적 복원이라 할 수 있다. 정성들여 선택한 300그루 이상의 나무와 수천 종의 식물, 그리고 수백 종의 각기 다른 캘리포니아 토착종이 이 프로젝트가 지향하는 풍요롭고 야심찬 식재 전략을 뒷받침하고 있다. 통바 파크와 켄 겐서 광장은 캘리포니아의 토착 식물들을 주요한 원예적 요소로 부각시키고, 최대 규모의 지중해식 초지 공원을 공공 공간에 제공한 최초의 대규모 프로젝트다.

기존의 수목들은 그대로 존치해 새롭게 식재된 식물군들을 뒷받침해주는 중추적 역할을 맡게 하였다. 산타모니카 주민들이 '모티'라는 애칭으로 부르는 커다란 무화과나무는 멋진 캐노피 덕분에 방문객들이 피크닉을 즐기기에 적당한 숲을 제공하고 있다. 세 그루의 다 자란 피쿠스 나무들은 '세 친구들'이라는 별칭을 갖고 있는데, 모티 근처에 성공적으로 옮겨 심어져 고속도로 소음 등을 상당 부분 차폐하는 효과를 거두고 있다. 또한 기존의 야자나무들은 공원의 주 출입구 근처에 무리를 이루도록 식재되어 공원 경계를 따라 수직적인 구조가 형성되었다.

새롭게 식재된 나무들은 크게 세 가지 형태의 숲을 이루도록 했는데, 이들은 각각 캘리포니아 해안 토착 관목, 수풀이 뒤덮인 지역, 그리고 강변 식물군을 모델로 하였다. 대상지의 다양한 미기후를 활용하고, 방대한 규모의 식재를 위한 틀을 제공하고, 또한 공원 내 독특한 개성을 지닌 공간을 구성하기 위해 매우 세심하게 식물 재료를 배치했다.

Water Bay. A scooped out bay along the park's central path is the backdrop for a sparkling waterfall sequence. Large boulders in front of the garden pool provide a visually delightful buffer, offer casual seating, and emphasize a relaxed informality.

발견의 언덕에는 공원 내 그 어떤 곳보다도 많은 나무가 식재되었다. 최대한 넓은 그늘을 확보할 수 있도록 은빛 올리브나무와 참나무류가 혼재되어 있다. 관찰의 언덕 부근에서는 소나무 숲을 만날 수 있다. 테라스식으로 구성된 관찰의 언덕 서쪽 경계는 남쪽을 바라보고 있으며, 공원 내에서 가장 척박한 환경을 가진 장소이기 때문에 블론드 앰비션 그라스를 비롯해 알로에 및 아가베 등을 혼합 식재하였다. 웨스턴 시커모어는 야생 잔디, 야생화, 지중해성 구근식물 등으로 이루어진 부드러운 초지 공간을 만들어내기 위해 습지의 언덕에서 저지대까지를 엮어 주듯이 식재하였다.

The rolling topography at Garden Hill provides an ideal surface on which to display grasses, succulents, aloes, agaves, and seasonal bulbs. These plants compose a public meadow garden of greater scale and complexity unseen in any other public space.

The park's Public Restroom is neatly tucked into the side of Observation Hill.

건축적 요소와 포장

건축적 요소들과 풍부한 질감의 포장 재료들은 공원이 지닌 무성한 초지 정원과 조화를 이루어 대상지가 지닌 '소협곡 물길'이라는 역사성을 강조하는 한편, 산타모니카의 독창적 공간을 위한 흥미로운 시각적 정체성을 만들어내고 있다.

벽과 길은 황금빛이 도는 현장 타설 콘크리트로 제작되었는데, 산타모니카 지역에서 확보한 각기 다른 크기의 골재들을 그대로 겉으로 드러냈다. 거대한 돌로 벽을 구성하고 이를 산책로 가장자리를 따라 간간이 배치하여 친밀하고 편안한 공간을 구성했다.

조개껍데기를 닮은 전망대는 공원 내 언덕 중 가장 높은 언덕 꼭대기에 자리 잡고 있는데, 산타모니카와 태평양을 내려다보는 멋진 조망을 제공한다. 전망대는 플라스마 컷 판금으로 제작되었으며, 커팅 패턴은 조경가가 제공한 3D 모델에서 직접 추출하여 사용하였다. 전망대는 은백색으로 마감하여 공원의 산책로, 벽, 그리고 초지 정원의 색깔인 풍부한 황금빛 색조와 보완을 이루도록 하였다.

알코브는 식재된 언덕을 파내어 오목하게 들어간 모양인데, 앉아서 사색을 할 수 있는 시설을 제공하기도 하고 자전거 거치대나 지역 주민들을 위한 사교 공간으로 활용될 수도 있다.

수경 시설들은 바다 쪽으로 흘러내려가는 단일한 물길을 통해 서로 시적으로 연결된다. 이들의 규모와 존재감은 주 출입구에 가까워질수록 점점 커진다.

부드럽게 대상지를 감싸 안는 조명은 방문객들이 언덕 위로 점차 올라감에 따라 확인할 수 있다. 밤이 되면, 통바 파크와 켄 겐서 광장의 조형적 형태와 얼기설기 엮인 산책로들이 은은하고 따뜻한 조명과 함께 방문객들을 맞이한다. 또한 조명은 공원의 입체적인 형태를 더욱 부각시켜 준다. 고효율 LED 및 HID 조명 시설이 공원과 광장 전역에 걸쳐 설치되어 있다.

지속가능성과 협업

이 프로젝트는 비슷한 규모의 다른 프로젝트들을 위한 새로운 지속가능성 모델을 제시하고 있다. 즉 환경적 요구와 문화적 요구를 세심하게 조화시킬 수 있는 방안을 제시한다. 토양 개선과 급격한 바이오매스 증가를 통하여 제공되는 강력한 생태계 복원은 공원 주변에 위치한 산타모니카 도시 빗물 재활용 시설로부터 가져온 물을 관개에 이용함으로써 비로소 완벽해진다. 관개에 사용된 물과 빗물은 공원 내 대부분의 언덕 기저에 자리 잡고 있는 바이오스웨일로 자연스럽게 이동하게 되므로 대상지를 벗어나지 않는다. 대상지 내 공간 중 식재가 이뤄지지 않은 곳들은 사회적 지속가능성에 기여한다. 시 정부 및 지역 사회와의 긴밀한 협력을 바탕으로 개발된 이 공원의 사회적 공간으로는 고요한 명상을 위한 공간, 넓은 주민 회합 공간, 그리고 모든 연령대 및 장애·비장애 방문객 모두를 포용하는 놀이 공간이 있다. 특히 통바 파크는 일련의 산책로, 자전거 이용 시설 등을 통해 이용자들의 건강을 증진시키는데, 공원 웹사이트를 통해서도 이에 대한 홍보가 이루어지고 있다.

프로젝트의 성공적인 실현과 높은 지속가능성을 가능하게 해준 것은 바로 도시, 지역 사회, 조경가, 다양한 분야의 전문 컨설팅 그룹, 그리고 디자인-빌드 업체로 구성된 프로젝트 팀의 완벽한 협업이었다.

번역 안호균

The Ocean Avenue Screen provides shaded
seating at the park's busiest corner.
Up-lighting on the screen highlights
its sculptural form and offers an added
sense of security at night.

Vincennes Zoo

Atelier Jacqueline Osty & associés

Landscape Design Atelier Jacqueline Osty & associés
Architectural Design of New Buildings
Bernard Tschumi Urbanistes Architectes with Véronique Descharrières
Architectural Design of the Technical and Renovated Buildings Synthèse Architecture with Bernard Hemery
Scenography of the Vivariums and the Park's Educational and Directional Sign-posting El Hassani & Keller
Technical Fluids Excluding the Pond-water Treatment SETEC Bâtiment
Other Technical Areas Bouygues Bâtiment-Île-de-France
Contracting Authority Groupement Chrysalis
Location Paris, France
Area
Overall surface 34.5ac
Greenhouse 43,000ft²
Atelier's Intervention 29.7ac
Bernard Tschumi Urbanistes Architectes Intervention 2.5ac
Planning 2008~2010
Completion 2011~2014
Photographs Martin Argyroglo, Claude Cieutat, Mikaël Mugnier

Paris Zoological Park

The Paris Zoological Park opened its doors again in April, 2014 after 27 months of renovation work that transformed it to the core while renewing the zoo's existing strong points, most notably the gardens' iconic Great Rock. 40% more landscaped space has been added to the original 1934 zoo, but most of all, it's the evolving vision of the relationship between humans and animals that has been completely revisited.

From Composition to Suggestion

From on-screen to off-screen, scenes from the wings, foreground and background, the eye is guided, and the views are infinitely receding, scripted meticulously in composition and framing. Continuing this metaphor, Atelier has created successive visual frames that enlarge the dimensions and break down distances between humans and animals. Time as a fourth dimension has been added to 2D and 3D. It becomes a part of how one perceives the zoo with permanently changing landscapes as we move through the seasons and years. And lastly, imagination acts as a fifth dimension where suggestion completes the mental landscape and rounds out this multi-scale composition.

Alternating overall views and total immersion, the circuit rolls out like a ribbon along which contrasting landscapes succeed each other. The zoo reactivates several landscaping devices that are traditionally used in garden art to reduce boundaries, frame views and hide certain elements. Topography is used as basic leverage to lead visitors from surprise to surprise without revealing the circuit's next stage. It is also a tool for enhancing the Great Rock, magnifying its 65m with an unparalleled low-angle shot.

Neither Here nor There

The biozones are not mere mimicry of idealized nature transposed to the heart of Paris. Atelier worked on suggestion, playing visual references—colors, matter, levels and surfaces—to steep visitors in the appropriate atmosphere. Landscapes have been completely invented with the original sites' essential features and relief being suggested. Thus the expanses of the Sahel and the empty plains of Patagonia are evoked by folding the ground and deploying the colors and matter specific to each place, the forests of Madagascar by the density and heights of its plant life. This dissimulation of tracks has led to the design of unique places through their landscapes, their spaces and their diversity. Visitors are neither "here" nor "there" but in an in-between world that generates a troubling disorientation.

Architectural envelopes

The vegetable matrix

The Discovery route

Encircled landscape according to biozones

The distribution of biozones

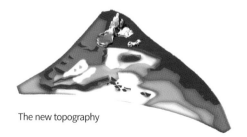

The new topography

The new Vincennes Zoo is thus composed of five biozones: Patagonia, the Sudanese Sahel, Europe, Guyana and Madagascar with a sixth, Equatorial Africa, to be completed at a later date.

Principle of composition of a Pens in an open environment

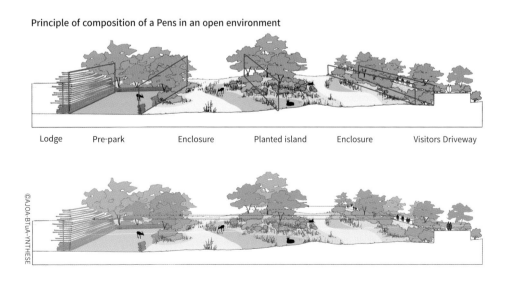

| Lodge | Pre-park | Enclosure | Planted island | Enclosure | Visitors Driveway |

The zoo reactivates several landscaping devices that are traditionally used in garden art to reduce boundaries, frame views and hide certain elements.

Patagonian landscape

Thwarting Nostalgia with a Radically New Proposal

Atelier's proposal consists in preserving the symbolic elements to counteract any temptation for nostalgia. The zoo has been organized around the Gardens' flagship landmark, the Great Rock. This was one of the brief's specificities and a strong point in Atelier's proposal. Renovated in the 1990s, it could be preserved as such, like certain other isolated rocks, ponds and trees.

On the other hand, rather than "sticking to the past," Atelier suggested a total remake of the landscaped spaces.

A zoo is a singular entity. In contrast to more traditional parks where the general public breaks down into well defined user groups(children, families, young people, the elderly, etc), each space in a zoo constitutes a distinct group with tailor-made treatment. In particular the agency developed the principle of fabricated landscapes, a dichotomy between the hidden and the visible, with specific attention paid to the wild animals.

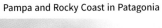

Pampa and Rocky Coast in Patagonia

117

Water tank for sea lions and seals in Patagonia region

Sahel-Soudan region

Five Biozones

Paris's Zoo Gardens are now composed of biozones that completely immerse the visiting public. The animals are no longer disconnected from their natural habitats but are shown as an integral part of the whole. Visitors are called upon to discover an enhanced landscape in which the visual, sound and olfactory surroundings increase the sense of a total change of scenery. The new Vincennes Zoo is thus composed of five biozones: Patagonia, the Sudanese Sahel, Europe, Guyana and Madagascar with a sixth, Equatorial Africa, to be completed at a later date. This doesn't mean that the natural spaces of an exotic region are merely imitated, for the landscapes through which visitors and animals circulate are suggested.

In developing a "mimetic" herbarium, Atelier selected plants similar to those endemic to the animals' regions. This didn't mean creating one landscape based on another but imagining an in-between world specific to the Vincennes Zoo. To reconcile Atelier's viewpoint with the animals' needs, the staff, the existing plant-life and the new features had to be constantly adapted and adjusted.

©Martin Argyroglo

Border of Madagascar and Guyana region

©Martin Argyroglo

119

Glasshouse in Guyana region

©Martin Argyroglo

Visitors are called upon to discover an enhanced landscape in which the visual, sound and olfactory surroundings increase the sense of a total change of scenery.

©Martin Argyroglo

2014년 4월, 뱅센 동물원이 27개월 만에 다시 문을 열었다. 정비 작업을 통해 파리 동물원 내부 정원의 상징이라 할 수 있는 그랑 로쉐르를 비롯한 주요 장소를 리뉴얼했다. 1934년 개장 당시에 비해 추가적인 조경 계획이 이루어져 총 면적 대비 40퍼센트 이상의 공간이 새로운 모습으로 탈바꿈했다. 무엇보다 인간과 동물 사이의 관계를 좀 더 발전적인 시각으로 검토했다.

암시와 연상의 경관

"사람들의 시야가 풍경이 펼쳐지는 화면에서 바깥으로, 장면의 끝에서 내부로, 전경에서 후경으로 옮겨가면서 경관은 무한히 먼 곳까지 확장되고, 마치 연극 대본처럼 세심하게 경관의 구성과 틀이 갖추어진다." 이 같은 메타포를 유지하면서, 인간과 동물 사이의 간극을 허물고 범위를 확장하는 연속적인 시각적 프레임을 만들어냈다. 2차원과 3차원에 시간이라는 새로운 차원이 도입된다. 이용자들은 끊임없이 변화하는 동물원의 풍경을 새로운 계절이 돌아오고 해가 바뀌는 시간의 흐름을 통해 인지하게 된다. 암시와 연상으로 대표되는 경관 구성 방식에 이용자들의 상상력이 더해지면 다섯 개의 차원에서 인지되는 다양한 스케일의 정신적 풍경이 완성된다.

디스커버리 트레일은 동물원을 전체적으로 조망할 수 있는 경관 포인트와 동물의 움직임 및 서식지 환경을 관찰할 수 있는 위요된 공간으로 구성된다. 서로 대비되는 성격의 공간을 교차시킴으로서 더욱 극적인 경험이 가능하다. 새로운 뱅센 동물원에는 정원 예술에서 전통적으로 이용되던 몇 가지 조경적 장치가 도입됐다. 이는 공간의 경계를 없애거나 경관의 틀을 만들기도 하며, 몇몇 요소를 숨기는 역할을 한다. 특히 지형을 이용해 디스커버리 트레일의 다음 단계를 보여주지 않도록 해 관람객을 놀라움의 연속으로 이끌 수 있도록 했다. 또한 이러한 지형 조건은 그 어디서도 경험할 수 없는 로우 앵글 숏으로 65m 높이의 그랑 로쉐르를 감상할 수 있게 한다.

중간 세계

뱅센 동물원의 바이오존은 단순히 이상적인 자연의 모습을 파리 한복판으로 옮겨 놓은 모방품이 아니다. 암시의 효과를 통해 고조되는 풍경을 제시하기 위해 색과 재료, 지형의 높낮이와 표면 등 시각적 재료를 이용했다. 관람객들은 점점 고조되는 경관을 경험하며 동물원의 새로운 분위기에 빠져든다. 바이오존의 여러 풍경들은 본래 생물대가 갖고 있는 특징에 관람객들의 연상이 더해져 더욱 완전한 모습으로 변화한다. 광활한 사헬-수단 지역과 파타고니아 고원의 넓은 초원은 각 장소에 알맞은 색과 재료의 배치를 통해 야생의 모습을 재현하고, 마다가스카르 지역의 숲은 크기가 거대한 나무를 밀식하여 아프리카 열대우림의 모습을 구현해냈다. 일부 숨겨져 있는 이동 경로는 각 지역의 풍경과 공간, 그리고 생물학적 다양성 사이를 넘나들며 다양한 경험을 제공한다. 동물원에서 시간을 보낼수록 도시도 아니고, 야생도 아닌 '중간 세계'라는 새로운 곳에 있다는 생각을 하게 될 것이다.

새로운 경관 조직 원리

정비 과정에서 동물원의 과거 모습을 상징적으로 보여줄 수 있는 요소만을 선별해 보존하는 방식을 채택했다. 오랫동안 동물원과 함께 했던 이들이 과거의 모습을 추억할 수 있도록 했지만, 과거의 모습을 모두 보존하려는 시도는 아니었다. 뱅센 동물원은 개장 당시부터 지금까지 내부 정원의 가장 핵심적인 랜드마크인 그랑 로쉐르를 중심으로 구성되어 왔다. 그랑 로쉐르는 설계 지침서에 구체적으로 언급된 여러 요소 중에 하나로서 아틀리에 자클린 오스티에서 제안한 설계안에서도 중요한 역할을 한다. 1990년 정비 작업 시 그랑 로쉐르는 홀로 고립된 다른 주요 바위나 연못, 나무처럼 고립되어 보존되었다. 그러나 아틀리에 자클린 오스티는 '과거에 집착하기'보다, 이전과는 전혀 다른 모습의 경관을 만들어내는 방안을 제안했다. 뱅센 동물원은 단일한 공간을 지향한다. 특히 관람 과정에서 보이지 않는 장소와 보이는 장소가 명확하게 구분되도록 경관 조직 원칙을 만들어왔다. 이는 동물원의 야생 동물에 더욱 집중할 수 있는 환경을 조성하게 했다.

다섯 개의 바이오존

뱅센 동물원의 내부 정원을 구성하는 바이오존은 방문객이 완전히 몰입할 수 있도록 조성되어 있다. 새로 조성된 바이오존은 동물들이 인공의 자연에 더욱 동화될 수 있도록 야생의 모습과 동물에게 필요한 것들을 최대한 반영하여 설계되었다. 관람객들은 동물원 곳곳에서 시각, 청각, 후각적 요소의 변화를 감지할 수 있어 더욱 풍부한 경험을 기대하게 된다. 뱅센 동물원의 바이오존은 파타고니아, 사헬-수단, 유럽, 가이아나 및 마다가스카르의 다섯 곳으로 이루어져 있고, 추후 적도 아프리카 지역이 완공되면 모두 여섯 곳이 된다. 가이아나 지역의 식물원을 구성하는 과정에서 더욱 사실적이고 충실한 식물 표본실을 만들기 위해 동물들이 서식하던 동물원 내의 고유의 식물 종과 유사한 식물이 선택되었다. 이 같은 설계 전략은 어떤 다른 풍경에 기초하여 한 풍경을 만들어내기 위한 작업이 아니라, 뱅센 동물원만 독특한 특징이 살아 있는 중간 세계의 풍경을 상상하게 만든다.

번역 손은신

Atelier Jacqueline Osty & associés has created successive visual frames that enlarge the dimensions and break down distances between humans and animals.

Group HAN

Baegot Ecological Park

Landscape Architects Group HAN
Construction SANGROK
Client Siheung City
Location Jeongwangdong, Siheungsi
Gyeonggido, Korea
Area 232,464m²(neighborhood park)
Completion 2015
Photographs
Yeong-Geun Lee, Cheong-O Yu, Group HAN

Baegot, from Salt Pond to New Town

Baegot New Town, where Okgudo Urban Nature Park and Siheung Neumnaegil are located, meets Walgot Port in the north, Oido Island in the south, and the Yellow Sea in the west. Originated from "Hangeul Baegot," a Korean language school founded by Si-kyoung Joo, a renowned Korean linguist, "Baegot" was selected as a brand name for the city. Consisting mostly of mud flat, the land was used to produce sundried salt in the 1970s. It went through reclaiming

Baegot Ecological Park serves
as an urban landmark where ecology and culture
stand side by side.

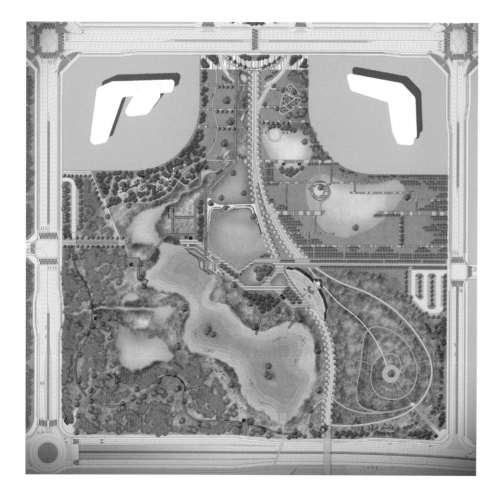

Constructed along the 6-kilometer-long beach,
Waterfront Park is designed to restore the
12-kilometer-long, dynamic coastline where
visitors can feel the delight of wind and waves.

work to be used as a gunpowder performance test site in the 1980s. During the 1990s, the surrounding areas began to be developed rapidly, resulting in the closure of the test site in the 2000s and initiating the comprehensive development process.

Symbolic Image of City Brand

The construction of a park as a new open space seemed to contribute to enhancing the living quality of Baegot New Town in Siheung and promoting the city brand. It was not desirable that the local government should become a sole player to participate in the development project, but, instead, the city residents could play a major role in building the park step by step over a long period time, which would work as a good example of engaging citizens in the development process of a futuristic, "user-oriented" park. Under the slogan of "Ecological City Siheung." We strived to construct a environment-friendly park, which could contribute to promoting the city both as "a city embracing humans" and "a city embracing nature." As a part of the differentiating strategies, we came up with a plan to make the best of the sea and mud flat, and constructed a habitat for various bird species, which enhances biodiversity.

The soil excavated from the digging process for the pond was retreated and reused for planting trees in the park.

©Yeong-Geun Lee

127

Memories of Old Coastline

Baegot New Town in Siheung is located on the reclaimed land, which used to be islands and mud flat in the west coast of the Korean peninsula. The site has much potential to remind visitors of their old memories. A gentle breeze that blows through the forest, trees that provide shades and shelters from the glowing sun, and undulating waves of the sea and meandering tidal channels are all great resources that the site used to possess. Baegot Ecological Park and Waterfront Park were designed to become friendly open spaces, restoring the memories of the site and offering citizens some opportunities to enjoy themselves in nature.

Design Concepts and Objectives

Reeds, islands, mud flat, docks, wind, fog, pine trees, and the glow of the setting sun are all considered as Baegot's emotional resources. Constructed along the 6-kilometer-long beach,

©Cheong-O Yu

As a model for a user-oriented and citizen participatory park, Baegot Ecological Park is designed to be developed and completed gradually, creating a futuristic image.

Waterfront Park is designed to restore the 12-kilometer-long, dynamic coastline where visitors can feel the delight of wind and waves. In addition, to create a distinct identity of Baegot New Town, Haesongsimni Boulevard is being constructed along Waterfront Park, and Hyanggimalli Boulevard along Neumnaegil.

Harmony of Nature and Humans

Located in the center of Baegot New Town, Baegot Ecological Park, the total area of which is 232.464m^2, is surrounded by Waterfront Park, commercial facilities, and cultural venues. With the core concepts of "life," "participation," and "culture," the park was developed by preserving the reed field and wet land, which constitute approximately 30% of its total area in order to conserve the existing ecosystem and landscape elements to the fullest. In addition, seawater ecology pond was created for the first time in Korea by using salt water and tides. The tides of the Yellow Sea pump the ocean water into the seawater ecology pond twice a day without any assistance from artificial power sources, creating brackish water zone together with rainwater collected within the site. This pond offers a unique habitat for different species of plants and animals, thereby enhancing biodiversity and promoting birds' feeding activities. The soil excavated from the digging process for the pond was not transported out of the site, but retreated and reused for planting trees in the park.

Passageway from the main entrance to seawater ecology pond. Huge open spaces are preserved near the lake for concerts, gatherings, and events. Around the main passageway are small elements for meetings and resting and stages for performances.

©Yeong-Geun Lee

Concrete pavement symbolizing
the holes in mud flat.

The young of gray mullets in the pond.
The ecology pond provides a unique habitat
created by brackish water zone.

Park that Develops and Grows with Citizens

Baegot Ecological Park is not like ordinary parks that are usually commissioned by clients and developed exclusively by designers, but it has been centered around "Baegot Forest School" since the earliest design stage. Not only have we strived to hear and understand the residents' ideas and opinions, we have also attempted to educate "citizen gardeners" and promote their professional competences, leading them to manage and maintain the park for themselves.
Due to these efforts, Baegot Ecological Park has become a respectable model for user-oriented open spaces. It is not a completed park yet, but there is still a plenty of room to be filled by the participation of the citizens over a long period of time, which we call "Citizens Participation Garden." A campaign was successful in encouraging both residents and businesses to donate funds or trees to the park, and the citizens themselves planted the trees to build green forest.

Baegotmaru, Baegot New Town's Observatory

Baegotmaru is a 29-meter-tall observatory, which was constructed to provide a panoramic perspective over Baegot New Town. Visitors can enjoy the landscape of the Yellow Sea, the sunset, and an attractive night view of Songdo. The spacious reed field and the silver grass trail surrounding the observatory are sure to become a landmark of Siheung.

The tides of the Yellow Sea pump the ocean water into the seawater ecology pond
twice a day without any assistance from artificial power sources.

Land of Life and Nature

Baegot Ecological Park has changed into a land of life and vitality which a variety of wild species inhabit, including some endangered ones such as narrow-mouthed toads and Korean Golden Frogs. Since its opening to the public, the park has been a welcoming open space in which visitors can pleasantly spend time in nature and children can enjoyably learn about ecology. Baegot Ecological Park will continue to offer a memorable experience and a leisurely atmosphere in the midst of the rapid transformation created by the new town development.

Translation Ho-Kyoon Ahn

Sky deck with a view of the lake and the surrounding landscape

배곧, 염전에서 신도시로

배곧신도시는 북측으로 월곶 포구와 남측으로 오이도, 서측으로 서해와 면해 있고, 옥구공원과 '시흥 늠내길'이 조성되어 있다. 한글 학자 주시경 선생의 한글 교육 장소인 '한글배곧'에서 창안하여 '배곧'이 도시 브랜드로 명명되었다. 1970년대에는 갯벌과 천일염 생산을 위한 염전으로 이용되었고, 1980년대에는 총포 화약 성능 시험장 용도로 매립되었으며, 1990년대에는 주변 지역의 개발이 본격화되어 2000년대에 화약 성능 시험장을 폐기하고 토지를 매입해 본격적인 개발을 시작했다.

도시 브랜드의 상징

시흥 배곧신도시의 삶의 질을 제고하고 도시 브랜드를 형성할 수 있는 새로운 오픈스페이스로 공원의 필요성이 대두되었다. 관의 일방적 주도가 아닌 시민과 함께할 수 있는 이용자 중심의 공원, 시민 참여형 도시 공원의 모델로서 단계적으로 만들고 완성하는 미래 지향적 방향이 요구되었다. '생명도시 시흥'이란 정신 아래 '인간을 품은 도시', '자연을 품은 도시'라는 개발 목표에 부합하고 자연 경관을 활용한 환경 친화적인 공원을 조성하고자 했다. 이를 위한 차별화(특화) 전략으로 바다(해수)와 갯벌을 활용하고 조류 서식처를 조성해 생물다양성을 보전할 수 있도록 했다.

Pedestrian bridge connected to the main path leads to Waterfront Park facing the Yellow Sea

Winding passageways among reed fields provide different views.

오래된 해안선의 추억

시흥 배곧신도시는 섬과 바다가 있던 서해를 도시 개발 사업에 따라 매립한 지역으로 대상지의 오랜 시간적, 장소적 기억을 되살리고 품어야 할 가치를 지니고 있다. 소나무 숲 사이로 속삭이며 부는 쾌적한 바람결과 내리쬐는 태양빛 아래 해변을 따라 시원한 그늘을 제공하는 숲, 굽이치며 일렁이는 파도와 드넓은 갯벌위 갯골의 살아 숨 쉬는 물결 등 오래된 해안선의 추억은 대상지가 가진 가장 큰 자원이었다. 배곧 생명공원과 수변공원은 이러한 대상지의 기억을 회복하고 시민들이 이용하기에 최적화된, 강한 정체성을 지닌 쾌적한 오픈스페이스로 조성하고자 했다.

설계 개념과 방향

갈대, 섬, 갯벌, 바람, 나루, 안개, 해송, 낙조 등 배곧의 감성적 자원을 도입했다. 6km의 해안을 따라 조성된 수변 공원은 바람결, 파도결을 따라 펼쳐지는 12km의 다이내믹한 해안으로 복원하고자 했다. 더불어 배곧신도시만의 정체성을 부여하기 위하여 수변 공원을 따라 해송십리海松十里 길을, 늠내길을 따라 향기만리香氣萬里 길을 계획했다. 해송십리, 향기만리 길을 비롯한 수변공원은 곧 완공될 예정이다.

자연과 사람의 공존

배곧신도시 중앙에 위치한 배곧생명공원은 주변으로 수변 공원, 상업 시설, 문화 시설과 인접하고 있으며, 면적은 232,464m²이다. '생명', '참여', '문화'를 콘셉트로 하여 기존 생태계와 경관 자원을 보존하기 위해 공원 면적 중 약 30%를 차지하는 갈대숲과 습지를 보존하여 개발했고, 국내 최초로 바닷물과 조수간만의 차를 활용하여 해수 생태 연못을 조성했다. 해수 생태 연못은 인위적 동력을 배제하고, 서해의 조수간만 차에 의해 하루 두 번 해수가 연못으로 자연스럽게 드나들게 한 습지로서 공원 내에서 집수되는 우수(담수)와 만나 기수역을 형성한다. 이렇게 조성된 공간에는 서식 환경이 각기 다른 동식물이 서식하므로 종 다양성을 풍부하게 하여 조류의 먹이 활동도 활발하게 한다. 연못을 조성하기 위해 터파기한 기존 갯벌 흙은 외부로 반출하지 않고 토양 개량하여 공원 내 식재토로 재활용하는 시도를 했다.

©Cheong-O Yu

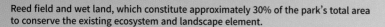

Reed field and wet land, which constitute approximately 30% of the park's total area
to conserve the existing ecosystem and landscape element.

시민과 함께 만들어가고 채워나가는 공원

배곧생명공원은 발주자 또는 설계자의 일방적 주도로 조성된 공원이 아니라 설계 초기 단계부터 '배곧숲학교'라
는 교육 프로그램을 운영했다. 시민의 의견을 단순히 듣고 수렴하는 단계에서 벗어나 '시민정원사'라는 조직을 육
성하고 전문가로서의 역량을 키워 직접 공원 관리와 운영을 맡게 했다. 이러한 노력 덕분에 배곧생명공원은 이용
자 중심의 공원으로 자리매김하고 있다. 완성된 형태의 공원이 아니라 오랜 시간 시민과 함께 완성해 나간다는
개념으로 '시민참여마당' 공간을 넓게 비워두었다. 일부 공간에는 수목 헌수 운동을 통해 시민과 기업들의 참여를
독려했고, 마련된 기금으로 시민들이 직접 수목을 식재하여 녹색 숲을 조성했다.

Along the traffic line leading
to the apartment complex is a children's
playground for family visitors and residents.

배곧신도시의 전망대 '배곧마루'

29m 높이의 배곧마루를 조성하여 배곧신도시의 전체적인 경관을 감상할 수 있는 전망대 역할을 하게 했다. 배곧마루에서는 서해의 경관과 낙조, 매력적인 송도 야경 등을 감상할 수 있다. 공원의 너른 갈대밭과 더불어 배곧마루 전체를 뒤덮고 있는 억새 둘레길은 시흥의 랜드마크로 자리매김할 것이다.

The spacious reed field and the silver grass trail surrounding the observatory are sure to become a landmark of Siheung.

137

자연이 살아 숨 쉬는 생명의 땅

배곧생명공원은 멸종 위기 동물인 맹꽁이, 금개구리 등을 비롯한 다양한 야생 동물이 서식하고 각종 새들이 날아와 휴식을 취하며 먹이 활동을 하는 생명의 땅으로 거듭났다. 개장 이후 평일, 주말 할 것 없이 많은 사람이 찾는 일상을 위한 공원으로, 아이들을 위한 생태 교육의 장으로 자리매김하고 있다. 신도시의 급격한 변화 속에서 메말라 가는 감수성과 여유를 선물하는 공원이 될 것이다.

Baegot Ecological Park will continue to offer a memorable experience and a leisurely atmosphere in the midst of the rapid transformation created by the new town development.

©Cheong-O'u

139

Busan Citizen Park

Yooshin + James Corner Field Operations

General Design, Landscape Architecture
Yooshin Engineering Co.(Man-Jae Yu, Seok-Gi Kim, Gyu-Hyun Jung)
Civil Engineering KHIL PYUNG Engineering Co.(Gi-Man Park, Hoe-Cheol Yun, Gyu- Hyeon Jeong)
Design Development James Corner Field Operations(James Corner, Jae-Yun Jeong)
Construction Hwasung Industrial Co.
Supervision Yooshin Engineering Co., KHIL PYUNG Engineering Co.
Client Busan Metropolitan City
Location 73, Simingongwonro, Busanjingu, Busan
Area 470,748m²
Completion 2014
Photographs Cheong-O Yu

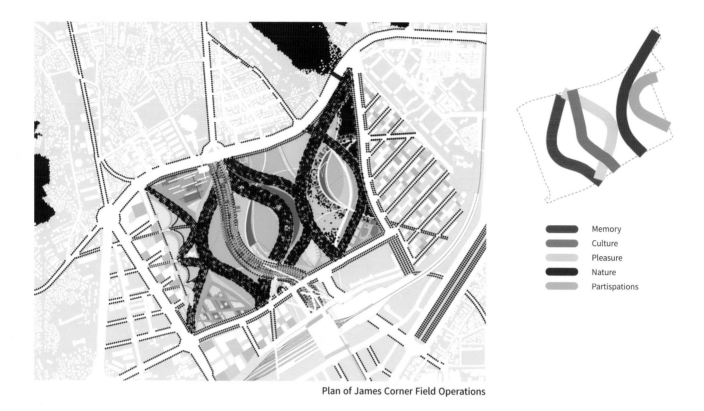

	Memory
	Culture
	Pleasure
	Nature
	Partispations

Plan of James Corner Field Operations

Return to the Citizens' Arms

Since the prehistoric to the modern era, Beomjeondong area, where the Citizen's Park is located, has long been the provider of livelihood for the local residents who used the well-developed farmlands for agriculture. However, in 1930, a racecourse built by the Japanese colonialists here at the outskirts of Busan eventually took away the farmlands; when the Sino-Japanese War broke out, the area was turned into a logistics base, and so began its history as a military site. Camp Hialeah was constructed after the end of the Korean War and functioned as the largest logistics support base in Korea that managed the transferring of goods and officers and men. Until its closure in 2006, its presence was detrimental to the formation of amenities required for living spaces and urban development in nearby region for approximately 50 years.

As the city expanded, the site, which originally sat on the suburbs, eventually became part of the city center. Multi-faceted reviews took place, including discussions regarding the demolition of the site. The idea of turning the site into a park was especially sought after—for the purpose of recovering amenities required for areas around the military base that has become a slum, and for the qualitative improvement of the city through securing urban open space not unlike the Central Park or the Hyde Park. Finally in 2004, it was decided that the site will become a neighborhood park; after several site standardization and adjustments in observation of the Regeneration Promotion Projects in underdeveloped areas nearby, the park finally came back to the arms of its citizens.

General Concept

Though the master plan and the working design was determined to be executed by Yooshin Corporation, the significance and the symbolism of the Citizen's Park was taken into consideration; as a result, an Invited Design Competition was held after series of consultations and public hearings. The design competition took place after selecting design firms—among the well-known foreign design firms—that were willing to participate. Finally, 'ALLUVIUM' by James Corner Field Operations was selected.

ALLUVIUM begins its narrative from the geographical location of the city of Busan. It reminds one of the rich history of the land by being located at the alluvial delta on the fertile river mouth of the Nakdonggang River. By selecting three spatial concepts and five program concepts through the meaning and the potential of ALLUVIUM, the design created a park endowed with new meaning and significance.

1. Memory Forest Walk
2. Cultural Forest Walk
3. Joyful Forest Walk
4. Nature Forest Walk
5. Participatory Forest Walk
6. Bujeon Stream
7. Mirror Pond & Tunnel Fountation
8. Lawn
9. Jeonpo Stream
10. Urban Beach

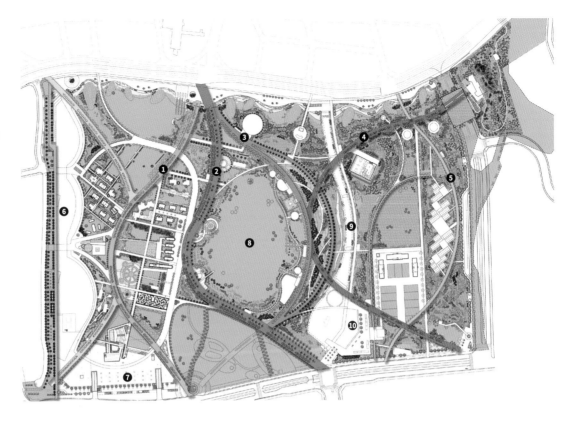

Master Plan

A large fountain and a tunnel fountain that made use of 25m-stainless steel was designed as landmark facilities near the park entrance.

Three Spatial Concepts: Flow, Accumulation, Connectivity

An alluvion is formed by flow of river and accumulation of soil, and makes way for connectivity between the river and the sea. The site has been an accumulative space whose flow had been suspended for the last century, as it was occupied by the U.S. Hialeah Military Base following the Japanese occupancy period. ALLUVIUM will penetrate the standstill flow of the city, revitalizing the river flow and recovering the ruptured flow of the greenery. Organic and dynamic system of movements will allow for easy flow and connectivity among parks, cultural facilities, commercial facilities, and infrastructure around the site. Two river streams present on our site, Bujeon and Jeonpo streams, previously covered, will be restored ecologically so that fresh water can flow. Ruptured green axis of Hwaji and Hoengnyeong mountains will be recovered through the wide forest pathways that run across the Citizen's Park.

ALLUVIUM will accumulate the memories of the new future upon the history of the past. Citizen's Park will be an open space where new forces flow in and accumulate memories and cultures, joys and nature, and citizens' participations, open to everyone. The significance of such accumulation begins by an accumulation of topography; a symbolic act. Sculptural land manipulation through fine accumulation of topographies will transform the large park site into a delicate multi-functional human-scaled space.

Diverse hierarchies and scales of the system of movements in and across the park convolve around the every nook and corner of the park, providing the optimum accessibility to everyone. Circulatory path around the park interior is created with a gentle slope without level differences, allowing everyone to enjoy the park without any difficulties.

Ginkgo trees were used as main species for the Memory Forest Walk.

©Cheong-O Yu

©Cheong-O Yu

Exhibition wall expressing history through images of waves

Five Program Concepts: Memory, Culture, Joy, Nature, Participation

Busan Citizen Park has been sectioned using the five conceptual forest pathways based on the five program concepts—memory, culture, joy, nature, participation—and the sub-pathways that cross the park inside and outside. Park elements were also organically connected.

Memory Forest Walk: This site was inaccessible to the citizens for the last hundred years as it was used as a racecourse and as a temporary military training center during the Japanese occupation and also during a half-a-century-long usage as U.S. military base. Memory Forest Walk will be a space where history of pain and scars are remembered as well as where layers of everyday memories accumulate to form a new future.

Park History Museum building was used as a race ticket booth during the Japanese occupation and as officers' clubhouse during the Camp Hialeah days; it is currently remodeled into a museum. Residence for non-commissioned officers was remodeled into an Art and Culture Village where exhibition, education and special programs have been installed. Trace Mall, previously barracks, was remodeled into convenience facilities. Furthermore, Historical Walkway and Wall of Memories that convey the history of Busan were constructed. Memory Colonnade is an illumination colonnade that makes use of wooden telegraph poles found within the base and forms symbolic landscape. Watchtowers and chimneys inside the base were recreated while disused oil tanks were reformed into sculptural benches. Exhibition wall that show the flow of history through images of waves makes useful playground for children.

Amusement facilities have been positioned
along the Forest Path.

Large-scale events and performances may be held on approximately 40,000m²-lawn.
Illumination tower have been installed.

Cultural Forest Walk: Busan Citizen Park serves as the city's new cultural center that hosts diverse cultural and artistic events, and will be a starting point for Busan in becoming a world-renowned cultural city. Cultural Forest Walk, along with the lawn plaza, is an open space where diverse forms of culture such as performance and events are shared. Illumination tower and 40,000m^2—lawn that may hold large—scale events and performance have been installed.

Joyful Forest Walk: By designing the entire Forest Walk with rubber chip pavement, safe environment for playful activities have been created. Circle towers appropriating its topography and use of facilities that meet the Barrier Free Certification requirements were introduced so that anyone and everyone may enjoy the space. Furthermore, royal azaleas hill below pine trees provide a different kind of visual pleasure. Outdoor stage that made use of the entrance to the theater building of the original military base was renovated, and renamed as "Trace Theater."

At the Joyful Forest Walk, tulips and flowering cherry were introduced to draw interest and attention, while rubber chip pavement design created safe environment for playful activities.

©Cheorg-O Yu

Memory Colonnade. Illumination colonnade using the wooden telegraph poles found within the U.S. Base

Nature Forest Walk: Sylvan greens and wide lawn, and seasonal landscapes will become a dramatic space that convey nature within our daily lives. Pine tree-lined road and diverse flowering plants that makes connection to the native forest belt add to the interesting landscape. Forest cafe was created, using the commander residence in the military base. Also, urban beach that relay the city's identity (as symbolized by Haeundae), music fountains and water parks draw the attention of its users.

Participatory Forest Walk: This park is a space that is shared by all of Busan's citizens; anyone living in Busan has a chance to share and own a piece of the park. Experience of ownership and cultivation will allow the park to become a familiar and significant participatory space for its citizens. In order to achieve this goal, three residential buildings for company officers have been remodeled into Park Cultural Center. Participation Wall, decorated with tiles holding the names of citizen donors have been created.

Furthermore, a large fountain and a tunnel fountain that made use of 25m-stainless steel was designed as landmark facilities near the park entrance. After sunset, illumination and laser shows using diverse colors and lights provide visual entertainment.

Translation Ho-Kyoon Ahn

Citizen's Park will be an open space where new forces flow in and accumulate memories and cultures, joys and nature, and citizens' participations, open to everyone.

다시 시민의 품으로

부산시민공원이 위치한 범전동 일대는 선사 시대부터 주거가 이루어질 정도로 농경지가 발달하여 근대에 이르기까지 농토로 이용하던 지역민의 삶의 터전이었다. 그러나 1930년, 당시 부산의 외곽 지역이었던 이곳에 일제에 의해 들어선 경마장은 삶의 터전을 앗아 갔고, 중일전쟁 발발과 함께 병참기지화 되어 군사 시설로의 역사가 시작되었다. 캠프 하야리아는 한국 전쟁 종전 후 설치되어 물자와 장병의 이동을 관리하는 대한민국 최대 군수 기지 역할을 하였으며, 2006년 폐쇄되기까지 50여 년 간 인근 지역의 도시 개발 및 생활권 기능 형성에 있어서 저해 요소로 작용했다.

더욱이 도시가 확장되자 도시 외곽에 자리했던 부지가 도심에 놓이게 되면서 철거 논의를 비롯한 다각적인 검토가 이루어졌다. 특히 슬럼화된 군 기지 주변 지역의 생활권 기능 회복과 더불어 센트럴 파크와 하이드 파크 등과 같이 도심 오픈스페이스 확보를 통한 도시의 질적인 발전을 위해 공원화를 모색하게 되었다. 결국 2004년 근린공원으로 최초 결정되었고, 주변 낙후 지역의 재정비촉진계획과 맞물려 부지 정형화 및 조정을 거쳐 현재의 시민공원 부지로 결정, 시민의 품으로 돌아오게 되었다.

기본 구상

부산시민공원에 대한 기본 및 실시설계는 (주)유신으로 결정되었으나, 시민 공원의 중요성과 상징성을 감안, 전문가 자문 및 공청회 등을 거쳐 인지도가 있는 해외사 중 참여 의사가 있는 설계사무소를 선정하여 지명 초청 설계공모를 실시하였고, 그 결과 제임스 코너 필드 오퍼레이션스의 '얼루비움' 안이 선정되었다.

얼루비움 개념은 부산의 지리적 위치에서 시작한다. 비옥한 낙동강 하구의 삼각주 충적지에 위치하여 번성한 땅의 역사를 되새겼으며, 얼루비움이 갖는 의미와 가능성을 통해 세 개의 공간 주제와 다섯 개의 활동 주제를 설정하여 새로운 의미의 공원을 조성하고자 하였다.

Urban beach relay the city's identity as symbolized by Haeundae.

©Cheong-O Yu

Mirror Pond

세 개의 공간 주제: 흐름, 쌓임, 연결

충적지는 하천의 흐름과 토양의 퇴적으로 형성되며, 강과 바다가 연결된다. 일제강점기를 거쳐 하야리야 미군 부대가 주둔해온 지난 한 세기 동안의 대상지는 흐름이 정지된 적체의 공간이었다. 얼루비움은 막혔던 도시의 흐름을 뚫어주고 갇혀있던 하천의 흐름을 되살리며 단절된 녹지의 흐름을 회복할 것이다. 유기적이고 역동적인 동선 체계는 부지 주변에 위치한 공원, 문화 시설, 상업 시설, 도시 기반 시설 간의 원활한 흐름과 연결을 가능하게 한다. 부지 내에 복개되어 있던 부전천과 전포천은 생태적으로 복원되어 맑은 물로 다시 흐르게 될 것이며 잘려나갔던 화지산과 횡령산의 녹지축은 시민 공원 내를 가로지르는 넓은 폭의 숲길늘에 의해 다시 회복될 것이다.

얼루비움은 이러한 과거의 역사 위에 새로운 미래의 기억을 쌓아갈 것이다. 시민 공원은 새로운 기운이 흘러들어와 기억과 문화, 즐거움과 자연, 그리고 시민의 참여가 쌓이는 모든 사람에게 열린 공간이 될 것이다. 이러한 쌓임의 의미는 지형의 쌓음이라는 상징적 행위를 통해 시작된다. 미세한 지형의 쌓음을 통한 조형적인 대지 조작은 거대한 공원 부지를 섬세한 휴먼스케일의 복합 공간으로 변모시킬 것이다.

공원 안팎을 가로지르는 다양한 위계와 규모의 동선 체계는 공원 구석구석을 감아 돌며 모든 이에게 최적의 접근성을 제공한다. 공원 내부를 도는 순환 동선은 단차 없이 완경사로 조성되어 모든 이들이 불편 없이 공원 곳곳을 감상할 수 있게 될 것이다.

다섯 개의 활동 주제: 기억, 문화, 즐거움, 자연, 참여

부산시민공원은 기억, 문화, 즐거움, 자연, 참여 등 다섯 개의 주제 숲길과 그 사이사이 공원 안팎을 가로지르는 다양한 보조 동선으로 공간을 구획하고 또 유기적으로 연계하였다.

Busan Citizen Park has been sectioned using the five conceptual forest pathways
based on the five program concepts and the sub-pathways that cross the park inside and outside.

기억의 숲길: 이 부지는 일제강점기 경마장과 일본군 임시군속훈련소, 반세기 동안의 미군 주둔지로 지난 100년 간 우리가 밟지 못한 우리의 땅이었다. 기억의 숲길은 아픔과 상처의 역사를 되새기는 동시에 일상의 기억을 겹 겹이 쌓아 나가며 새로운 미래를 만들어가는 공간이 될 것이다.

공원역사관은 일제강점기에는 마권발매소로 미군 주둔 시절에는 캠프 하야리아의 장교 클럽으로 사용된 건축물로, 지금은 리모델링하여 공원역사관으로 조성하였다. 하사관 관사는 문화예술촌으로 리모델링하여 전시와 교육, 체험 프로그램을 도입했다. 흔적 몰은 막사를 리모델링하여 편의시설로 조성되었다. 그밖에 부산의 역사를 담은 역사의 길 및 기억의 벽을 조성했다. 기억의 기둥은 부대 내 목재 전신주를 활용한 조명 열주로 상징적 경관을 연출하였다. 또 부대 내 망루와 관사의 굴뚝을 재현하였고, 폐 유류 탱크는 조형 벤치로 재탄생했다. 흘러가는 역사를 물결의 이미지로 표현한 전시 가벽은 아이들에게는 좋은 놀이시설이 된다.

문화의 숲길: 부산시민공원은 다양한 문화예술 행사가 열리는 부산의 새로운 문화 중심지이며 세계적인 문화 도시로 거듭나기 위한 시작점이 될 것이다. 잔디광장과 어우러진 문화의 숲길은 공연, 행사 등 문화를 공유하는 열린 공간이다. 대규모 행사 및 공연이 가능한 약 40,000m^{2}의 잔디광장 및 조명타워를 설치했다.

Historical Walkway that convey the history of Busan

©Cheong-O Yu

©Cheong-O Yu

즐거움의 숲길: 숲길 전체를 고무칩 포장으로 설계
하여 안전하게 뛰어놀 수 있는 공간을 조성하였다.
지형을 활용한 사면놀이 등의 서클타워, 배리어 프리
인증 기준에 부합하는 놀이 시설 도입으로 누구나 함
께 즐길 수 있는 공간을 제공하였다. 더불어 소나무
하부에 펼쳐진 철쭉동산은 또 다른 시각적 즐거움을
선사한다. 기존 부대 내 극장 건물의 출입구를 활용
한 야외무대는 '흔적극장'이란 이름으로 재탄생했다.
자연의 숲길: 우거진 녹음과 넓은 초지, 사시사철 변
하는 경관은 우리 생활 가장 가까이에 자연을 안겨주
는 극적인 공간이 될 것이다. 기존 수림대와 연계한
소나무 가로수길과 다양한 초화는 경관적 흥미를 더
한다. 부대의 사령관 관사를 활용하여 숲 속 카페를
조성하였다. 더불어 해운대로 대표되는 부산의 정체
성을 반영한 도심 내 백사장 조성과 음악분수, 물놀
이장으로 이용객의 흥미를 유발하였다.
참여의 숲길: 이 공원은 부산 시민 모두가 공유하는
공간이며 부산 시민 누구나 공원의 한 자락을 나누
어 소유할 수 있는 기회를 가진다. 소유와 가꿈의 체
험을 통해 공원은 시민들에게 더욱 친근하고 소중한
참여의 공간으로 다가가게 될 것이다. 이를 위해 위
관급 관사 세 개동을 리모델링하여 공원문화센터를
조성했고, 시민 헌수자 이름이 새겨진 타일로 장식된
참여의 벽을 조성하였다.
이외에도 공원 진입부의 랜드마크 시설로 높이 25m
의 스테인리스 스틸 구조물로 만든 대형 분수와 터널
분수를 설계하였다. 야간에는 다양한 색채의 조명과
레이저 쇼를 연출하여 볼거리를 제공한다.

Tunnel Fountain

155

DONGSIMWON Landscape Design & Construction

Gyeongui Line Forest Park

Yeonnamdong Section
Design Development DONGSIMWON
Landscape Design & Construction +
LUL(Seoul University Department of
Landscape Architecture and Rural
Systems Engineering Landscape Urbanism
Laboratory, Professor Wook-Ju Jeong,
Jong-Ho Won, Hyuk-Jun Jang, Jae-Hyuk
Choi)
Construction Document DONGSIMWON
Landscape Design & Construction
Length 1,310m
Area 28,500m²
Completion 2015

Yeomnidong Section
Design DONGSIMWON Landscape Design &
Construction
Length 160m
Area 4,820m²
Completion 2015

Saechanggogae Section
Design Development DONGSIMWON
Landscape Design & Construction +
Sungkyunkwan University Endowed Chair
Professor Sung-Ryong Jo
Construction Document DONGSIMWON
Landscape Design & Construction
Length 630m
Area 19,580m²
Completion 2015
Photographs Cheong-O Yu

Yeonnamdong section

©Cheong-O Yu

158

Past and Present

Gyeongui Line Forest Park is a 6.3km trail park created along the old Gyeongui Line. It covers approximately 101,700m² with the width that varies from 10 to 60m. The track had been a busy pathway for people and goods, connecting Mapo and Yongsan long before the railroad was built. However, since 1970s, its importance began to diminish as the alternative transportation took its part. As the city grew, the railway dissecting the city areas was regarded as a polluting factor harming the quality of lives, and the adjacent areas became slums. Since then, the area shunned by the people began to be shaped uniquely and differently from other metropolitan areas.

Construction plan

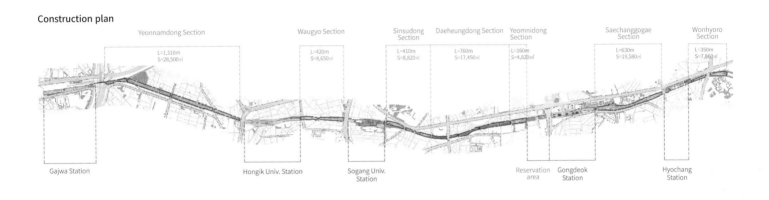

Yeonnamdong Section
L=1,310m
S=28,500㎡

Waugyo Section
L=420m
S=8,650㎡

Sinsudong Section
L=410m
S=8,820㎡

Daeheungdong Section
L=760m
S=17,450㎡

Yeomnidong Section
L=160m
S=4,820㎡

Saechanggogae Section
L=630m
S=19,580㎡

Wonhyoro Section
L=350m
S=7,860㎡

Gajwa Station

Hongik Univ. Station

Sogang Univ. Station

Reservation area

Gongdeok Station

Hyochang Station

Triangular pond at the intersection with Donggyoro. Symbolic measure for Songjang Stream and the railway above it that once were but now paved up.

©Cheong-O Yu

159

Forest trail and the green field at the mouth of Yeonnamdong Section. Two types of concrete pavement were applied.

Open area in Seongmisanro intersection. An open area was created with sleeper and rails, sagoseok, PC concrete in the mid part of Yeonnamdong Section.

Design Concept and Strategy

For the physical design process, the historic, local, social and ecological considerations were taken to be the most valuable elements. With the geological characteristics of the site, the emphasis was given to realize these elements most effectively with matching spacial structures, lines of movements, materials and forms. Rather than using the old railways, the materials were de-constructed and reconstructed partially and indirectly to create various stories which will bring visitors' attention and help them find their own discoveries about the site.

The other emphasis was on the fact that the railway has been the wall that dissects and blocks adjacent areas. Because most of the railways were about 5 to 10m higher above the ground,

©Cheong-O Yu

Yonsu underground passage. Once the most secluded corner in Yeonnamdong has now become the most vibrant place with the trail and a new 2-lane street.

the few tunnels underneath the railways permitted people to travel across the railway. The transformation of the railways into a park created new vitality in the area. Three strategies were established to make the park into a place of communication and exchange. First one was to connect streets into the park. Secondly, by planning the main trail to zigzag, the matching curves met the streets to form junctions. The third was to create the open spaces for the community along the zigzag trail.

Yeonnamdong Stream.
The concrete pavement was hard-edged;
on the edge of the non-paved trail, aquatic
plants were established to form a natural.

©Cheong-O Yu

Pond, the source of Yoennamdong Stream.
Underground water from 50m underground is
supplied to form Yoennamdong Stream.

Benches and grass fields were established along the trail at various places
for visitors to relax and listen to the stream.

©Cheong-O Yu

163

Yeonnamdong Section

Yeonnamdong Section of Gyeongui Line Forest Park extends from Hongik University to Hongjecheon(stream) covering 1.31km with the average width of about 25m. This section is most populated with relatively easy access and has vibrant communities nearby in Yeonnamdong and Donggyodong. The most unique characteristic of this section is water stream. Underground water pumped from the new underground Gyeongui Line is supplied to form a stream in the park. Development of a new commercial area by the new subway station might look too overwhelming; however, the stream created with underground water provides ecological counterbalance. With an old ginko forest in the adjacent community, this part has the most impressive landscape in the Yeonnamdong Section.

Yeonnamdong community open area. Wide-open grass areas were created for the people in the communities to create their own spaces.

Yeomnidong Section

Yeomnidong Section is only 160m long, the shortest of all. However, it is somewhat wide with the average of 31m and has a relatively flat terrain. Near the park are many offices with great pedestrian flow, and the construction of a major multiplex cinema is on the way. In the past, salt trade flourished in this area though no trace of it is to be found today. To bring back the historic memory of the section, templates and stories boards were put up to tell the history of Mapo, Gyeongui Line and Yeomnidong.

Saechanggogae(ridge) Section

Saechanggogae is a ridge connecting Hyochangdong and Dohwadong. The name originated from a new warehouse(Saechang), Manrichang built during Chosun dynasty. The Gyeongui Line created a valley cutting up the Yongsan mountain range. The deep valley was created by filling up more than 10m to develop a natural green flow back again. On the slope, step terraces were created to form a new locality mixing up the past and the present. **Translation** Ho-Kyoon Ahn

Yeonnamdong open area with pergola. A rest area resembling a platform with parallel line on the pavement reminds of old railway.

©Cheong-O Yu

165

경의선의 어제와 오늘

경의선숲길은 총연장 6.3km의 경의선 철길 폐선 부지에 조성된 선형 공원으로 공원 구간의 면적은 약 101,700m², 폭원은 10~60m다. 마포와 용산 일대를 횡단하는 이 길은 열차가 다니기 훨씬 이전부터 많은 사람과 물자가 왕래하던 활발한 교통로였다. 1970년대 이후 운송 수단의 발달로 인해 점차 그 중요성이 약화되기 시작했다. 도시화가 진행되면서 이 도심 속 철길은 생활 환경을 저해하는 주범으로 낙인 찍혔고 주변 지역은 자연스럽게 슬럼화되었다. 하지만 낙후된 철길은 경의선 주변 마을이 일반적인 도시 지역과 다른 지역성을 갖게 하는 계기가 되기도 했다.

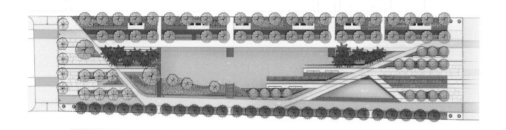

Yeomnidong Section

Yeomnidong grass area and trail. Open spaces were created for the community activities.

©Cheong-O Yeo

168

설계 개념과 전략

공원의 물리적 구현 과정에서 역사성·지역성·사회성·생태성을 가장 우선적으로 고려해야 할 가치로 설정하고, 공간의 지리적 특성을 반영하여 각각의 가치를 효과적으로 구현할 수 있는 공간 구조, 동선 체계, 재료, 형태를 모색했다. 철길의 형태를 그대로 적용하기보다는 재료를 해체하고 재구성하는 간접적 재현 방식을 통해 방문객의 관심과 발견을 유도하여 다양한 이야깃거리를 만들고자 했다. 또 다른 이슈는 철길이 오랜 시간 동안 지역 커뮤니티의 소통을 가로막는 장벽이 되었다는 점이다. 경의선은 대부분의 철로가 주변보다 5~10m가량 높게 솟아 있기 때문에, 토끼굴 형태의 길을 통해서만 철로를 지나다닐 수 있었다. 공원 조성은 마을의 숨통을 트는 새로운 기회가 되었다.

공원 조성을 통한 소통의 확산 효과를 극대화하기 위해 세 가지 전략을 세웠다. 첫째, 공원으로 향하는 주변 골목길을 공원을 통해 이어주는 것이다. 둘째, 공원의 주 보행 동선을 지그재그 형태로 계획하여 동선의 절곡부와 주변의 마을길이 만나는 결절점을 만드는 것이다. 셋째, 지그재그 산책로 사이에 만들어지는 넓은 공간을 커뮤니티 오픈스페이스로 남겨두는 것이다.

연남동 구간

경의선숲길 연남동 구간은 홍대입구역부터 홍제천까지 이어지며, 길이는 1.31km, 평균 폭은 약 25m다. 경의선숲길 중에서 가장 유동 인구가 많고 접근이 쉬운 지역으로, 연남동과 동교동 일대의 커뮤니티도 잘 유지되고 있는 곳이다. 이곳의 가장 큰 특징 중 하나는 물길이다. 경의선을 지하화하면서 발생한 지하 용출수를 지상부로 끌

Yeomnidong mirror pond.
Aquatic elements are supplied to bring vitality.

어울려 공원길을 따라 흐르도록 했다. 지하철을 중심으로 한 복합 역사 개발이 자칫 과도하게 여겨질 수 있지만, 지하철 때문에 발생한 지하수를 지상부에서 활용함으로써 공원의 생태성을 높이는 효과를 볼 수 있다. 지역 공동 주택 근처에 보존되어 있는 은행나무 수림대는 그대로 활용해 연남동 구간의 가장 인상적인 경관이 되도록 했다.

염리동 구간

염리동 구간은 160m로 길이는 이번 사업 구간 중 가장 짧지만 31m 폭의 비교적 넓은 평지형 구간이어서 이용 가치가 높다. 공원 주변에 크고 작은 오피스들이 위치하여 직장인의 이동이 많고, 공원에 인접하여 대형 주상복합 단지가 건설되고 있기 때문에 앞으로 많은 시민이 이용할 것으로 기대되는 곳이다. 옛날에는 이 지역에 염전, 소금창고, 시장이 번성했지만 지금은 그 흔적을 찾아보기 어렵다. 경의선숲길 염리동 구간에는 지역의 옛 장소성을 회상할 수 있는 장치로 마을 이야기 안내판을 설치해 염리동과 마포의 역사, 경의선의 역사를 기억할 수 있도록 했다.

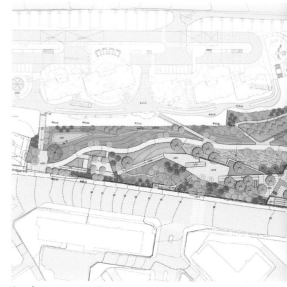

Saechanggogae Section

Yeomnidong zelkova walkway. Cozy resting place for office workers nearby.

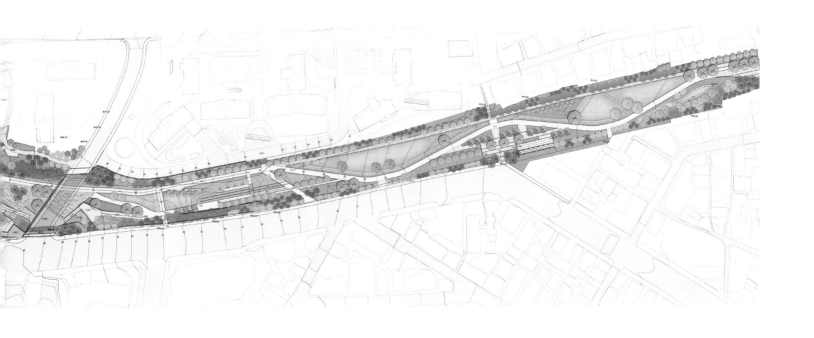

Yeomnidong railway garden. Herbaceous flowers in between rails and stones create a unique space.

©Cheong-O Yu

171

Railway intersection.
A railway intersection was recreated.
It was a pathway to work and school
for the people in the community
for tens of years.

Remains of the old railway.
Some of the railway was reconstructed.
Next to the old concrete retaining wall,
a rest area was created.

Open area with stones and woods in Saechanggogae Section. Step terraces connecting to the slope can be used for various purposes like resting area, exhibitions and community meetings, etc.

New apartments and the park replaced
the railway in Saechanggogae Section

©Cheong-O Yu

새창고개 구간

새창고개는 효창동에서 도화동으로 넘어가는 고개로, 고갯마루 근처에 조선 시대 선혜청의 새 창고인 만리창을 지었던 데서 그 이름이 유래되었다. 경의선 철길이 놓이면서 협곡이 발생하여 수십 년간 용산 지맥의 흐름이 단절되어 있었다. 새창고개 구간에 경의선숲길을 조성하면서 깊게 파여 있던 계곡을 10m 이상 성토하여 녹지의 흐름이 연결되도록 했다. 경사면에는 다단형 테라스 공간을 조성하여 과거와 현재가 중첩되며 새로운 장소성이 생겨나도록 계획했다.

Yongsan mountain range of Saechanggogae Section.
Bed rock was found during the construction of the park,
and the plan was altered to accommodated the bed rock, which confirms that
Yongsan range flows all the way to Han River through Saechanggogae.

©Cheong-O Yu

Group HAN

Hwaseong Dongtan Cheonggye Central Park

Landscape Architects Group HAN
Construction KUNLIMWON
Client Korea Land & Housing Corporation
Location Seokudong, Bansongdong,
Dongtanmyeon, Hwaseongsi, Gyeonggido,
Korea
Area
Overall surface 213,724m²
Landscape Architecture 153,902m²
Completion 2015
Photographs
Seung-Myeong U, Cheong-O Yu

Recognition of Time and Order

Under the slogan of "Intimate Dongtan," we strived to build an attractive and distinctively Korean city image of Dongtan New Town II, representing its local identity filled with affection and excitement. To do this, we came up with a Korean model of urban parks by constructing Korean-style villages based on the reinterpretation of traditional villages and traditional landscape architecture with an introduction of the theory of Yin-yang and five elements of the universe. Originally, the topography of the site was characterized by the fact that it is high in the east and relatively low in the west, with the hills and forest in the east leading to Mt. Banseok located in Dongtan New Town I. Small creeks and streams go through every corner of the villages and forests, flowing into Anseong and Chidong Stream, and winding streets of the villages lead to small factories and towns. Along the village streets is a landscape, which embraces Mt. Mubong and Mt. Banseok of Dongtan New Town I.

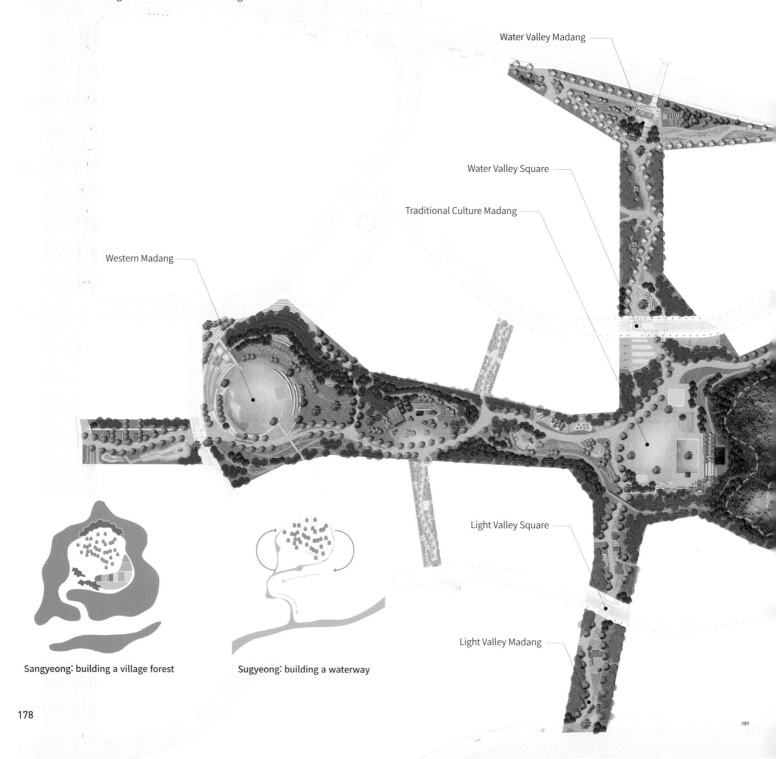

Water Valley Madang

Water Valley Square

Traditional Culture Madang

Western Madang

Light Valley Square

Light Valley Madang

Sangyeong: building a village forest

Sugyeong: building a waterway

When we visited the project site, most of the area seemed flat except for some preserved land surrounded by Mt. Mubong and Mt. Banseok, and Rivera CC and Chidong Stream. In addition, the site had a sense of place to an extent that it could become a center of the community as it was surrounded by apartment houses, schools, and commercial facilities.

Design Concepts and Objectives

Based on the understanding of mountains and water, traditional villages are composed of both physical and ecological elements such as a variety of gardens and winding roads. This provides an experiential landscape where you can enjoy the view of the mountain over the fence of your garden and the beautiful scenery sitting at a pavilion. By inheriting the ecological and cultural meanings of traditional villages and reinterpreting them as contemporary values, we developed the four core design concepts of Sangyeong, Sugyeong, Sugi, and Seunggyeong, with which we came up with a comprehensive design, constructing a sustainable, green infrastructure.

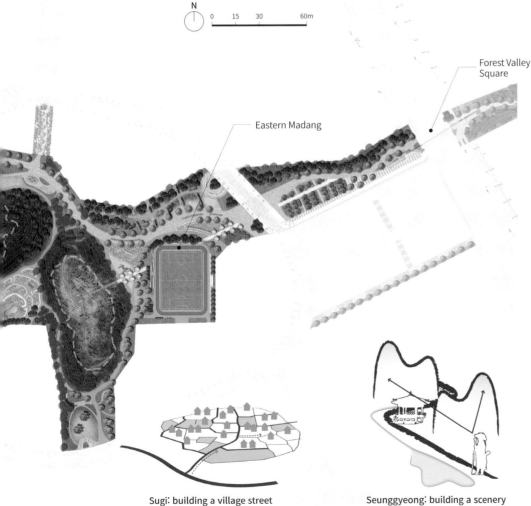

N

0   15   30   60m

Forest Valley Square

Eastern Madang

Sugi: building a village street

Seunggyeong: building a scenery

Sangyeong, building a forest that protects a village: With a motive of a hill and a village forest that used to be common in the project site, we designed a hilly park constructing a three-dimensional landscape. Considering the context and characteristics of vegetation, we built various types of village forests, designing a regional green network. The three-dimensional land is a part of the green network originating from Mt. Mubong, working as an ecological foundation. It also serves as a cultural foundation for madang and relevant programming in a close connection with the environment. The village forest located on the three-dimensional land consists of four types. The east-west green network is a traditional village forest, where

In the center of Western Madang is a circular lawn.
On the low mound in the east of the lawn is a stone stand, in front of which is a small stage.

Waterscape facilities representing the cultural functionalities the puddles
and washing places of traditional villages used to have serve as a center of community activities.

A bridge in Western Madang not only connects the mounds but works as a landmark highlighting the park's entrance.

pine, oak, and zelkova trees are planted representing the prominent vegetation of Mt. Mubong and the preserved land, creating a multilayered colony. Along the south–north green network, loose–lower hornbeams and maple trees are planted to protect the privacy of residents and enhance scenic beauty.

Sugyeong, building a healthy waterway: Traditional villages are equipped with a natural water cycle system, which enables surface water and rainwater to go through streams and creeks into rice paddies and rivers, purified. Following this tradition of wisely utilizing rainwater, we employed an efficient rainwater management system that allows for the permeation, collection, and utilization of rainwater within the park. A natural drainage system was designed to take advantage of rainwater according to the basin of each section. The rainwater collected from green fields and pavements flow into vegetation watercourses, rainwater gardens, and grass waterways first, and then it is reused as supplementary water for waterscape facilities. If excessive rainwater is collected, overflow pipes lead the water into the existing rainwater pipelines. We created waterscape facilities representing the cultural functionalities that the puddles and washing places of traditional villages used to have.

Sugi, building a communicative village street: The spatial hierarchy of traditional villages consists of streets and gardens. Based on this concept, we planned different small alleys connected to the apartment houses and schools in the adjacent areas to strengthen the connectivity to the center of the city. In addition, gardens are constructed along the small alleys at the major spots in the park. We also designed the community activities centered around these gardens and alleys, making them the hubs of local communities. A thematic circular pathway in the back of the village connecting viewing points and hills is divided into a upper trail and a lower one.

Seunggyeong, building a scenery at every step: The back alleys of the village, where people can take a walk on a hill and through a forest, provides a variety of scenic experiences depending on different altitudes. The landscape created by Mt. Banseok, Dongtan New Town I, and Mt. Mubong can be enjoyed within the site thanks to the method of borrowed scenery. Park features such as a toilet at the entrance and a bridge in the park play a symbolic role and work as landscape elements.

Introduction of the theory of Yin–yang and five elements of the universe: According to the character of the land and the directions of Yin–yang theory, a sense of place is created and species of trees are selected for street trees. The colors of ground cover plants and flowers of shrubs are also chosen carefully to create a symbolic landscape. The reinterpretation of tradition including the image of traditional villages, functionality based on usability, and considerations for the harmony among various facilities are all included in the comprehensive design planning.

Application of traditional methods and materials: Reinterpreting the traditional method of stacking up stones, we constructed gabions made of wood and steel, which are placed at various locations in the park. Traditional paving materials of soil, arch–stone, and tile contribute to empowering the concept of the Korean tradition and making the site environmentally friendly. Furthermore, the paving materials are highly permeable.

A thematic circular pathway and a topography playground are located between Cultural Heritage Madang and Learning Madang

Experience-oriented play space is constructed with the reinterpretation of the Korean cultural heritage.

©SeungMyeong U

Madang

Large-scale madangs including Western Madang, Traditional Culture Madang, and Eastern Madang, and Entrance Madang, Learning Madang, and Channel Madang are located at the major spots in the park, highlighting the symbolism of the Korean park.

Western Madang: Passing through the small entrance leading to the regional business complex, visitors will see sculptural mounding, a toilet, and a hill on a bridge. Open lawn and ecology pond, with a village as a background, enhances the symbolism of the park. This is designed to serve as a local community space closely connected to the streets in the neighborhoods.

Traditional Culture Madang: A large lawn madang and a small madang are designed to accommodate a large-scale event and small-sized gatherings or meetings respectively. It contributes a lot to creating a Korean image of the space to employ traditional landscape architecture elements such as a small palace, Bangjiwondo, and Hwagye. To secure the viewing points toward Mt. Banseok, a small palace, the preserved land, and a bridge connecting hills are all closely interconnected to create a circular pathway.

Eastern Madang: To increase the multi-functionality of the park, the playground of a nearby elementary school is constructed in the park. Forest Valley Madang located around a mirror pond and a flower garden is connected to the commercial facilities so as to work as an open street park, which will likely boost community activities.

Channel Madang: This is connected with Chidong Stream in the north of the site. We constructed the water network connected to the stream and the water-friendly environment. Flowers and a colony of pine trees are planted to strengthen a sense of entrance.

Translation Ho-Kyoon Ahn

You can enjoy the views of Mt. Banseok and Dongtan New Town I.

시간과 질서의 깨달음

'정감情感 동탄'이라는 슬로건 아래, 동탄2신도시에 정과 흥이 넘치고 지역 고유의 정체성을 담은 매력적인 한국적 도시 이미지를 구축하고자 했다. 이를 위해 전통 마을을 재해석한 한국적 마을 만들기, 자연과 상생하는 음양오행 사상을 도입한 전통 조경의 재해석을 통해 한국적 도시공원의 모델을 제시했다. 대상지는 본래 동고서저의 지형으로 동쪽 무봉산 자락의 구릉과 숲이 동탄1신도시의 반석산을 향해 흐르는 광역적 녹지 체계를 갖추고 있었다. 숲과 마을 곳곳을 실핏줄처럼 흐르는 물길은 다랭이논과 둠벙을 통해 안성천과 치동천으로 향하고, 굽이치는 마을길은 소규모 공장과 마을로 이어진다. 마을길을 따라 펼쳐지는 풍광은 무봉산과 동탄1신도시의 반식산을 대상지 내로 끌어들인다.

답사 당시, 대상지는 동서로는 무봉산~반석산, 남북으로는 리베라CC~치동천을 연결하는 십자 형태의 구릉과 숲 속의 원형보존지 일부를 제외하고는 평지로 조성되어 있었다. 또한 공동주택, 학교, 상가에 둘러싸여 있어 지역 공동체의 기반이 될 수 있는 장소성을 지니고 있었다.

설계 개념과 방향

전통 마을은 산과 물에 대한 이해를 바탕으로 다양한 마당과 굽은 길 등 물리적 · 생태적 구성 요소로 이루어진다. 이는 대청마루에 담 너머 앞산의 풍경을 끌어들이고 정자에서 풍광을 감상할 수 있는 체험적인 경관을 제공한다. 전통 마을의 생태적 · 문화적 의미를 계승하고 현대적 가치로 재해석해 네 가지 설계 개념인 산경山徑, 수경水經, 수기修己, 승경勝景을 이용한 통합적 설계를 통해 지속가능한 한국적 그린인프라를 재현하고자 했다.

산경, 마을을 보호하는 숲 만들기: 과거의 대상지에서 볼 수 있었던 구릉과 마을숲을 모티브로 입체적인 대지를 조성해 한국적 구릉형 공원을 계획했다. 주변 현황과 식생 구조를 고려한 다양한 유형의 마을숲을 조성해 동서축과 남북축을 이루는 광역적 녹지 네트워크를 계획했다. 입체적으로 조성된 대지는 무봉산에서 발원한 녹지축으로, 연속성을 갖는 생태적 기반이다. 또한 주변과의 관계를 고려한 마당 및 연계 프로그램을 위한 문화적 기반 요소로 활용되기도 한다. 입체적인 대지 위에 조성된 마을숲은 4가지 유형으로 구성됐다. 동서 녹지축은 전통 마을 숲으로, 무봉산과 원형보존지의 식생(소나무, 상수리 군락)과 전통 마을숲의 우점 교목인 느티나무, 소나무를 주 수종으로 하는 다층 구조의 군락이 식재됐다. 남북 녹지축에는 주변 주거 단지의 프라이버시와 경관을 고려해 서어나무, 단풍나무 군락이 조성됐다.

©Cheong-O Yu

This is the smallest madang of all,
located in the north of Bangjiwondo.

186

©Cheong-O Yu

We created a Korean image of the space by employing traditional landscape architecture elements such as a small palace, Bangjiwondo, and Hwagye

Event Madang. Madangs of various sizes are constructed to accommodate different events.

©Cheong-O Yu

수경, 건강한 물길 만들기: 전통 마을은 중수와 빗물이 여울이 있는 수로와 지당을 지나며 자연정화되어 논과 하천으로 흘러가게 하는 효율적인 자연 수순환 시스템을 갖추고 있다. 빗물을 지혜롭게 활용했던 이 수순환체계를 계승하여 공원 녹지 내 우수를 침투, 집수, 활용할 수 있는 빗물관리저감 기법을 도입했다. 지역에 따라 유역을 구분해 우수를 활용한 자연형 배수 체계를 계획했다. 녹지, 보도 등에서 유출된 빗물은 1차적으로 식생 수로, 빗물 정원, 잔디 수로로 유입되고 저류조를 통해 수경 시설의 보충수로 활용된다. 과도한 빗물이 유입되면 월류관을 통해 기존의 우수 관로로 물이 흘러가도록 했다. 전통 마을의 둠벙, 빨래터 등의 문화적 기능을 활용한 친수형, 경관형, 생태형 수경 시설을 조성했다. 이는 커뮤니티 활성화를 위한 거점 공간으로 활용된다.

수기, 소통하는 마을길 만들기: 길과 마당으로 구성된 전통 마을의 공간 위계를 모티브로 삼았다. 공원 내에 주변 토지이용계획(공동주택, 학교 등)의 고샅과 만나는 고샅길을 조성해 도심과의 연계성을 강화했다. 공원의 주요 공간에 고샅길을 중심으로 한 마당을 조성했다. 이를 바탕으로 한 고샅길 커뮤니티를 계획해 지역 공동체 허브의 기반을 마련했다. 또한 경관 포인트와 구릉을 연결하는 마을 뒷길인 순환형 테마 산책로를 낮은 길과 높은 길로 나누어 조성했다.

승경, 걸음 따라 즐기는 풍광 만들기: 구릉과 숲 속을 거닐 수 있는 마을 뒷길은 높이 변화에 따른 다양한 경관 체험을 제공한다. 또한 누각, 정자를 중심으로 하는 차경 기법을 통해 반석산, 동탄1신도시, 무봉산을 대상지 내로 끌어들였다. 공원 입구의 화장실, 브리지 등의 시설물은 공원의 입구성과 상징성을 강조하며 경관 포인트로 활용된다.

음양오행 사상의 도입: 땅의 품성과 음양오행 사상의 방위에 따라 장소성을 부여하고 이에 맞는 가로수를 테마 수종으로 선정했다. 지피 식물과 관목의 꽃 색깔도 오방색과 일치하도록 수종을 선정하고 식재하여 상징 경관을 연출했다. 전통 마을의 이미지를 고려한 전통성의 재해석, 실용성을 생각한 기능성, 시설물 간의 조화를 고려한 경관성을 감안한 토털 디자인 계획이 이루어졌다.

전통 기법과 재료의 적용: 전통 담장의 막돌쌓기를 현대적으로 재해석해 개비온을 만들었다. 철재와 목재로 만들어진 개비온을 다양한 형태로 응용하여 공원 곳곳에 설치했다. 한국적 콘셉트에 어울리는 흙 포장, 박석 포장, 전돌 포장 등 전통 기법과 친환경 포장재를 도입했을 뿐만 아니라 투수성이 높은 포장재를 선정했다.

A thematic circular pathway in the back of the village connecting viewing points and hills is divided into a upper trail and a lower one.

Following tradition of wisely utilizing rainwater, we employed an efficient rainwater management system that allows for the permeation, collection, and utilization of rainwater within the park.

When it rains, rainwater flows down through the stepped garden into the pond in the bottom and then is reused as supplementary water source.

마당

서녘마당, 전통문화마당, 동녘마당 등의 대형 마당과 입구마당, 배움마당, 물골마당 등 공원의 주요 공간에 위계감 있는 마당을 계획하여 한국적 공원의 상징성을 강조했다.

서녘마당: 광역 비즈니스 콤플렉스와 연결되는 좁은 입구를 지나면 조형 마운딩과 화장실, 브리지를 활용한 구릉이 펼쳐진다. 마을숲을 배경으로 개방형 잔디마당과 생태 연못인 동구연못을 조성해 공원의 상징성을 제고했다. 공원 주변의 생활 가로와 연계성이 강화된 지역 커뮤니티 공간으로 계획했다.

전통문화마당: 공원 중심의 커뮤니티 공간으로서 대형 이벤트를 위한 잔디마당과 소규모 모임을 위한 소규모 마당을 계획했다. 누각, 방지원도, 화계 등의 전통적인 조경 요소를 도입해 한국적 공간 이미지를 구현했다. 반석산을 바라볼 수 있는 조망축을 확보하기 위한 누각과 원형보존지, 구릉을 연결하는 브리지를 설치하여 순환 산책로를 확보했다.

The water features not just provide a chance to play with water, but also highlights the entrance of the park along with a colony of pine trees in the background.

Pine and oak trees in the preserved land are making a natural flow toward Eastern Madang,
and Zelkova trees and a variety of shrubs are planted as street trees.

©Cheong-O Yu

The waterway is connected to the ecology pond,
creating a water network with Chidong Stream in the north.
In the east of Water Valley Madang are a small garden and a stone stand.

동녘마당: 학교 시설 복합화 사업과 연계하여 인근 초등학교의 운동장을 공원에 설치해 셰어링파크를 실현했다. 미러폰드와 초화원을 중심으로 하는 숲골마당을 주변 상가와 연계하여 열린 가로 공원으로 계획했다. 이로 인해 커뮤니티가 활성화될 것으로 기대된다.

물골마당: 대상지 북측의 치동천과 연결되는 공원의 진입 공간이다. 치동천과 연계되는 수계축을 만들고 계류와 생태 연못 등의 물길 친화형 커뮤니티를 도입했다. 또한 화계 조성과 소나무 군식을 통해 입구성을 강조했다.

193

Part 2.

CAMPUS

Surfacedesign

IBM Honolulu

Landscape Architects Surfacedesign
Lead Designer James A. Lord
Landscape Architect of Record Helber
Hastert & Fee
Client Victoria Ward, Limited, Subsidiary of
Howard Hughes Corporation
Location Honolulu, Hawaii, USA
Completion 2013
Photographs Marion Brenner

Providing new ways of engaging with the architecture, the courtyard design pays homage to Ossipoff's façade pattern in the paving of its ground plane and in a new elevated water feature. The original landscape was never fully realized, and until this redesign Ossipoff's beautiful building sat in an asphalt parking lot. As viewed from the new Lanai—a vernacular Hawaiian landscape typology—the subtly articulated courtyard allows for flexibility for events and everyday use, ultimately creating a place of respite from the urban edge. The linear water feature screens the foreground while creating a linkage to the ocean's horizon line and reflecting the play and ephemerality of light throughout the day. Paving patterns reveal three dynamic qualities of the same volcanic stone, rooting the site in Hawaii's geologic origin. The stone's surface treatments—honed, which catches the light of the sky, flamed, which appears matte but shimmers when viewed from above; and split-faced, which exposes rugged depth—are expressed through the patterned courtyard, and register the transforming light through the day and night.

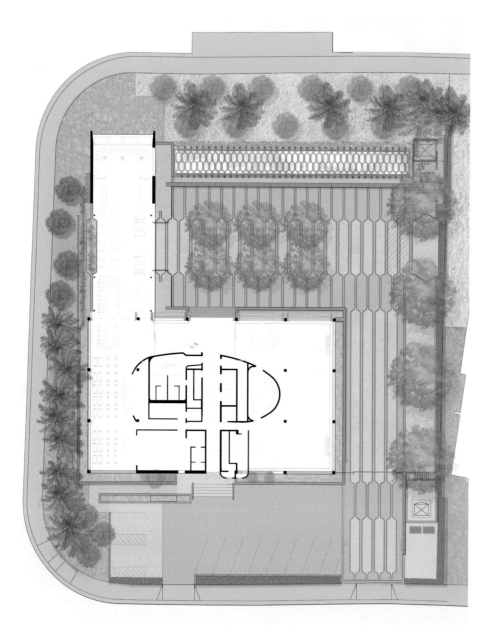

Master Plan

198

Located on busy Ala Moana Boulevard, the water feature forms a new horizon line connecting the courtyard to the beach, as the trickling water sounds mask traffic.

Scalar shifts in the patterning throughout the site allow users to discover new ways of engaging with the architecture and the site at large. The hardscape interweaves with permeable, native "lawn board" plantings, referencing the paradigmatic surfboard array at the beach's edge and speaking to the ecological history of the site.

Beyond rooting the design in the historical and visual context of the existing building, the landscape celebrates Hawaii's creation myth to create a space that speaks to the cultural history as well. The landscape architects met with native Hawaiian descendants to help articulate physical expressions of this sacred oral history. In the traditional Hawaiian narrative, people descend from Earth Mother and Sky Father, whose earthly children were first Taro, and then Man—created to care for Taro. The mysticism of this creation story is dynamically expressed through the patterns of water and light as the Sky Father is projected through the glass bottom of the water feature onto the Taro plantings and Earth Mother below.

The subtly articulated courtyard allows for flexibility for events and everyday use, ultimately creating a place of respite from the urban edge.

The courtyard tells the story of the literal ground it sits on. Three surface treatments(honed, flamed and split-faced) are expressed through the abstracted language of the courtyard.

The water feature—an elevated datum—is a visual
and experiential connection to the site's
context and an expression of the surrounding
sea and ever-changing island sky. Providing
new ways of engaging with the architecture,
the water feature showcases moving
reflections of light that capture the façade
and project it as a new dynamic horizon
line for the site that bridges landscape and
architecture. Automobile noise and paving
are obscured by this audible and visual
screen. The waves of the beach beyond Ala
Moana Boulevard seem to crash directly
onto the water's surface. The water reflects
its architectural muse and the sky during the
day and at night it transforms, emphasizing
the pattern of its steel runnels.

The architectural patterning integrates
further as water spills into a moat that
wraps the space, creating an illusion that the
courtyard floats in the sky. The moat is fed
by the cascade of scuppers dancing along
the elevated fountain edge.

Three contrasting textures are revealed
as the Hawaiian sun interacts
with the courtyard paving.

The minimalist palate of plants and stone expresses a distillation of the materiality and plantings of the surrounding Hawaiian landscape. The distinct Hawaiian sunlight is translated through different mediums— water, glass, metal, and living materials. Harnessing the dynamic environmental context, the courtyard design registers the sunrise, sunset, rain, and ephemeral quality of the Hawaiian light. The landscape is the first contemporary design in Hawaii to showcase all native and endemic plant species, educating visitors about Hawaiian ecologies in an urban context. As such, the design sets the stage for future development of the Victoria Ward that engages natural, historical and cultural histories of Hawaii.

©Marion Brenner

Native grass turf forms scaled "lawn boards" interwoven in the courtyard hardscape and function as permeable soakage features that allow water to percolate into the water table.

©Marion Brenner

The plaza expresses an abstraction of the building pattern, creating long boards in the paving pattern.

At the sunset hour, the courtyard is awash with a pink glow of the parting sun.

건축과의 새로운 소통 방법을 제시하는 중정 디자인은 지반면 포장과 새로운 고가 인공 수로를 통해, 블라디미르 오시포프가 창조한 건물 파사드 패턴에 대한 경의를 표하고 있다. 원래의 경관을 제대로 감상하기란 거의 불가능한 일이었으며, 이번 재설계가 있기 전까지만 하더라도 오시포프가 설계한 이 멋진 건물은 그저 아스팔트 주차장 안에 덩그러니 서 있을 뿐이었다. 하와이에서 유래한 독특한 베란다·파티오 형태인 라나이에서 바라보면, 세밀하게 표현된 중정이 다양한 행사와 일상적 용도에 두루 활용할 수 있을 만큼 충분한 유연성을 갖고 있으며, 궁극적으로는 도심에서 살짝 벗어나 한숨 돌릴 수 있는 공간을 제공한다. 전경을 가로지르는 직선형의 인공 수로는 바다에 펼쳐진 수평선과 연결되는 한편, 하루 동안 끊임없이 변화하는 햇빛의 발랄함과 덧없음을 반사되는 빛을 통해 표현하고 있다. 포장 패턴은 화산석이 지닌 세 가지 역학적 특성을 고스란히 드러내는데, 대상지가 하와이의 지질힉직 특질과 떼려야 뗄 수 없는 권게임을 다시금 싱기시커준다. 암석의 표면 처리 가운데 연마의 경우 포징면이 하늘에서 내려오는 빛을 제대로 붙잡아둘 수 있도록 해주고, 열처리의 경우 포장면은 광택을 띠지 않지만 높은 곳에서 내려다보면 반짝이는 특성을 지니게 한다. 또 암석을 쪼개 표면이 꺼칠꺼칠하도록 가공한 경우에는 다부진 깊이감이 나타난다. 이러한 세 가지 특성 모두가 패턴화된 마당 전역에 걸쳐 표출되고 있는데, 덕분에 밤낮으로 변모하는 빛의 모습이 여실히 드러나게 된다.

Providing new ways of engaging with the architecture, the water feature showcases
moving reflections of light that capture the façade and project it as a new dynamic horizon
for the site that bridges landscape and architecture.

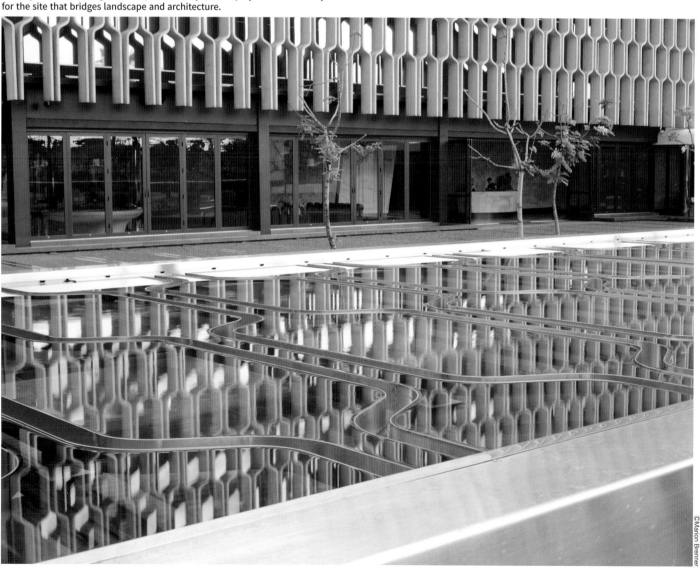

©Marion Brenner

대상지 전역의 패턴에서 나타나는 스칼라적 변화 덕분에 이용자들은 건축물을 비롯한 외부 공간과 소통할 수 있는 새로운 방법을 발견하게 된다. 인공적 조경 요소들은 투수성이 있는 토종 '잔디판' 식재와 절묘한 조화를 이루며, 해안가에서 흔히 볼 수 있는 나란히 늘어선 서프보드들의 모습을 연상시키는 한편, 대상지의 생태적 역사를 웅변하듯 보여준다.

설계 방향을 기존 건물이 지니고 있는 역사적, 시각적 배경과 일치시키는 것에서 한 걸음 더 나아가, 경관을 통해 하와이의 창조 설화를 보여줌으로써 문화적 역사 또한 함께 드러낼 수 있는 공간을 만들려 했다. 조경가들은 하와이 원주민의 후손들을 만나 구전으로 내려오는 성스러운 이야기를 어떤 방법을 통해 물리적으로 표현할 수 있을지 고민했다. 하와이 전통 설화에 따르면, 인간은 '어머니 대지'와 '아버지 하늘' 사이에서 태어났는데 그 첫 번째 자식이 타로(열대 지방에서 자라는 천남성과의 여러해살이풀)였으며, 타로를 돌보기 위해 인간이 창조되었다고 한다. 이러한 창조 설화를 물과 빛의 패턴을 통해 역동적으로 표현하고 있는데, 아버지 하늘은 인공 수로의 유리 바닥을 통해 그 아래쪽에 위치한 타로 식재와 어머니 대지 위로 투사된다.

©Marion Brenner

Materials, light and sound converge to create a dynamic edge that encapsulates the architecture of Ossipoff and the mythical heritage of Hawaii.

인공 수로는 대상지와 그곳이 지닌 배경을 시각적, 실험적으로 연결하기 위해 기획되었으며, 주변을 둘러싼 바다와 끊임없이 변화하는 하늘을 표현하고자 하였다. 건축물과 교감할 수 있는 새로운 방법을 제시하기 위해, 인공 수로는 반사를 통해 건물 전면의 모습을 포착하여 움직이는 빛의 형태로 보여준다. 이처럼 대상지에 새롭게 만들어진 역동적 지평선은 경관과 건축물을 하나로 통합시키는 역할을 한다. 자동차 소음과 도로 포장은 이러한 시청각적 벽에 가로막혀 그 정도와 형태가 완화된다. 알라 모아나 대로 너머에 위치한 해변의 파도는 마치 인공 수로의 수면에 직접 다가와 부딪치는 것처럼 보인다. 인공 수로의 불은 낮 동안에는 건축물과 하늘을 반사해 보여주고, 밤에는 새로운 모습으로 변신하여 수로를 둘러싼 강철 도랑의 패턴을 강조해 드러낸다. 건축 전체에 분포하는 일관된 패턴이 한층 더 강화되는 것은 물이 아래쪽에 위치한 해자로 떨어질 때인데, 이 해자가 공간 전체를 감싸 안으면서 중정이 하늘에 둥둥 떠 있는 듯한 착각을 자아낸다. 마치 춤을 추듯 배수구에 떨어지는 물 덕분에 해자는 충분한 수량을 확보할 수 있게 된다.

Inscribed runnels of stainless steel and glass frame ever-changing reflections, as water trickles down into a lush taro garden.

The pattern integrates further as water spills into a moat that wraps the space, creating an illusion that the courtyard floats in the sky.

미니멀리스트적인 감성이 드러나는 식물과 석재의 선택을 통해 물질성의 정화를 보여주는 동시에 주위를 둘러싼 하와이 고유 경관 속에 자리 잡은 식물들을 표현한다. 하와이의 햇빛이 지닌 독특한 개성은 물, 유리, 금속 그리고 살아있는 소재 등 다양한 매개체를 통해 해석되어 표현된다. 역동적인 주변 환경을 적절히 이용할 수 있도록, 외부 공간 디자인에는 일출, 일몰, 강우 그리고 하와이 햇살의 점멸하는 특성 등이 충분히 반영되어 있다. 대상지의 경관은 하와이에서는 최초로 시도되는 현대적 디자인으로서, 하와이의 모든 토착 및 자생 식물종을 망라해 보여주고 있다. 방문객들은 도심 속에서 하와이의 생태에 대해 배울 수 있는 값진 기회를 갖게 될 것이다. 나아가 향후 이를 바탕으로, 하와이의 자연사, 역사, 문화사를 간직한 빅토리아 워드 지역을 개발할 수 있는 토대를 마련하게 되었다. **번역** 안호균

At dusk, the magic moment, the polarized glazing of Ossipoff's building reflects multiple color spectrums across the surface of the water.

SLA
Novo Nordisk Nature Park

Landscape Architects SLA
Building Architects Henning Larsen
Architects
Climate Adaption Engineer Orbicon
Engineer Alectia
Landscape Contractor Skælskør
Anlægsgartnere
Biotopes Urban Green
Client Novo Nordisk
Location Bagsværd, Denmark
Area 31,000m²
Design Period 2010~2011
Completion 2014
Photographs Torben Petersen & SLA
Architects

In the city of Bagsværd, North of Copenhagen, Novo Nordisk has erected its new corporate headquarter. The headquarter, which houses the company's top management and 1,100 administrative staff, is located in a large, public park, designed by SLA Architects. The focus of the designers has been on maximizing the park's value for Novo's employees. Thus Novo Nordisk Nature Park not only provides Novo Nordisk with a green, recreational framework between its two new buildings; it also provides new and nature-filled opportunities for knowledge sharing, human dynamics, synergy and creativity.

Modern research has shown that people become more informal, more relaxed and more creative and open to new ideas when they are outside. This is especially true when they walk in nature that is wild, untamed, natural and varied in its expression.

Thus, in Novo Nordisk Nature Park this knowledge is used to create a lush nature park with a maximum of different, dense biotopes intersected by a winding path system cutting in, out and in-between the many different types of nature in the park. The park thus accentuates the aesthetic experience of nature, and is tailored to provide the greatest sensuous variation of light, shadow, smell, colours and sounds.

The paths wind up and down through the park's topography and in and out of biotopes to create maximum spatial variety. The paths of course provide general access around the site and from one building to another; but they also make it convenient for employees to meet their

colleagues and arrange walk-and-talk meetings outdoors. The paths never lead the shortest way from A to B, but wind their way between the biotopes in order to make each trip long enough for the employees to think creative thoughts and meet others on their way. Wild nature, crooked trees, chance meetings with colleagues, bird song and rosy cheeks all has become a natural part of the everyday working day at Novo Nordisk.

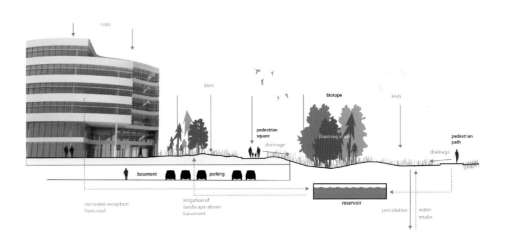

Water circulation plan

Novo Nordisk building entrance

The nature park itself uses a wide palette of native plants and holds over 1,000 new trees which over time will grow into clearly defined small "forests" and self-regulatory biotopes. The vegetation is designed to be wild and take care of itself which allows the biotopes to evolve with natural succession and minimal care. Because of the designer's stated desire to create maximum biodiversity in the park, several dead trees have been placed in between the newly planted trees. Dead tree trunks have vital value for natural ecosystems, as they are important habitats for beetles, caterpillars, mosses, etc. But they also provide the park with the smell of decay, the rot of the trunks and a direct confrontation with the life and death of nature's ecosystem. A powerful exhibition of the full aesthetic feeling of nature.

Sunlight will allow the vegetation and the leaves to cast weaving shadows on the gleaming white concrete of the paths.

©Torben Petersen & SLA Architects

The promenade was designed to be a meandering way to allow staff to walk leisurely and exchange enough without having the shortest distance between buildings and buildings.

The nature park's 1,000 trees are all inspected and hand-picked by the designers in specially selected nurseries, and composed in relation to their natural habitat, their shape, their volume and in relation to the local microclimate to maximize shelter for the users of the park and for the office buildings. The trees also help to absorb all rainwater that falls on site. Depressions are planted with alder trees and other water tolerant species in order to contribute to the park's ambitious climate adaption design. As such, Novo Nordisk Nature Park is the first park in Scandinavia with 100 percent natural water balance. Thus all rainwater that falls in the area and on the buildings is collected and used for irrigation. Because of the landscape's carefully designed topography and plantation the nature park can handle even torrential 100-year rainfall events without directing any water into the sewers.

Lighting also plays an integral part in the design of the nature park. During daytime, the sunlight will allow the vegetation and the leaves to cast weaving shadows on the gleaming white concrete of the paths. In the evening the landscape is lit up by carefully aligned tones of white light which highlights and enhance the natural colors and movements of the vegetation. Some biotopes are enlightened from within by varying Gobo light projections that create the atmosphere of shifting moonlight.

All in all, Novo Nordisk Nature Park provides Novo Nordisk with a strong, new landscape brand, while employees, clients, the citizens of Bagsværd and the local wildlife all have received a sensuous and lush landscape that provides room for recreation, inspiration, social meetings and a stress free environment all year round.

코펜하겐 북부의 박스베어드 시에 있는 노보 노르디스크 사는 새로운 사옥을 세웠다. 다국적 제약 회사인 노보 노르디스크의 최고 경영진과 1,100명의 직원들은 혁신과 지속적인 발전이 필수적으로 요구되는 치열한 경쟁 시장에서 일하고 있다. 따라서 노보 사의 직원을 위해 공원의 장점을 최대한 살리는 데 주력했다. 두 동의 새로운 건물 사이에 직원들의 휴식을 위한 녹지 공간을 조성해 사람들이 교류하고 지식을 공유하면서 창의적인 아이디어와 시너지 효과를 창출할 수 있게 했다.

공원의 전반적인 설계 개념은 산책을 하면서 자신의 사상을 발전시킨 키에르케고르나 니체와 같은 위대한 철학자에게서 영감을 받았다. 최근 연구에 따르면, 실내에 있을 때보다 야외에 있을 때 사람들의 행동이 훨씬 더 자유롭고 정신이 이완되어 새로운 아이디어가 샘솟는다고 한다. 특히 길들여지지 않은 야생의 자연 속을 거닐 때 효과가 극대화된다고 한다. 이러한 연구를 바탕으로 구불구불한 산책로가 여러 갈래로 교차하고 다양한 생물이 서식할 수 있는 비오톱이 무성하게 조성된 거친 자연 공원이 만들어졌다. 이 길들은 공원의 다양한 여러 자연 요소를 구획하며 그 사이를 누빈다. 이를 통해 사람들이 자연의 아름다움을 만끽하고 빛과 그림자, 향기, 색채, 소리와 같은 여러 감각의 변주를 최대한 감상할 수 있도록 세심하게 조성되었다.

Space created for employees to have lunch and tea outside

산책로는 공원의 지형을 따라 위아래로 구불구불하게 이어지며 공간의 다양성을 극대화하기 위해 비오톱 사이 사이를 누비고 있다. 이 길은 공원의 진입로일 뿐만 아니라 한 건물에서 다른 건물로 이동하는 경로도 된다. 또한 길은 직원들이 동료를 만나고 산책을 하며 야외 회의를 하기에 편리하도록 조성되었다. 길은 한 지점에서 다른 지점까지의 최단 거리를 잇지 않고 오히려 비오톱 사이를 굽이굽이 누비도록 되어 있다. 직원들이 산책하는 동안 동료를 만나고 창의적인 생각을 할 수 있을 만큼 충분히 긴 여정을 만들어내기 위해서다. 야생의 자연, 구부러진 나무, 동료와의 우연한 조우, 지저귀는 새소리 등 이 모든 것은 노보 노르디스크의 일상적인 업무의 일부로 자연스럽게 녹아들고 있다.

The paths wind up and down through the park's topography and in and out of biotopes to create maximum spatial variety.

The dead wood, which is a key habitat for beetles, larvae and moss, was placed on the biotope.

공원에는 다양한 종의 자생 식물과 천 그루가 넘는 나무들이 식재되었다. 야생화와 자생종을 식재함으로써 최소한의 유지·관리로도 비오톱이 자연스럽게 성장할 수 있도록 했다. 생물 다양성을 최대한 보존하기 위해 몇 그루의 죽은 나무도 새로 심은 나무 사이에 배치되었다. 고사목은 자연 생태계에서 중요한 가치를 지닌다. 딱정벌레, 애벌레, 이끼 등의 중요 서식지가 되기 때문이다. 또한 이 고사목이 서서히 썩어가는 냄새를 통해 사람들은 자연 생태계의 삶과 죽음의 모습이 어떤 것인지 직접적으로 대면할 수 있게 된다.

공원에 조성된 천 그루의 나무는 서식처, 수형, 크기 등을 세심하게 검토해 공원의 각 구역의 미기후에 맞춰 식재했다. 또한 이 나무들은 우수를 전부 흡수하는 데 일조한다. 공원의 기후 적응력을 높이기 위해 우묵한 땅에는 오리나무와 내수성이 강한 여러 수종을 식재했다. 이러한 설계를 바탕으로 한 노보 노르디스크 네이처 파크는 자연적인 수분 수지를 100% 달성하는 스칸디나비아 최초의 공원이다. 공원과 건물에 내리는 우수는 모두 집수되어 관개용수로 사용된다. 세심하게 설계된 지형과 식재 덕분에 세차게 퍼붓는 폭우에도 하수관으로 물을 전혀 내보내지 않고 강우량을 처리할 수 있다.

Area entering the park from the building

©Torben Petersen &SLA Architects

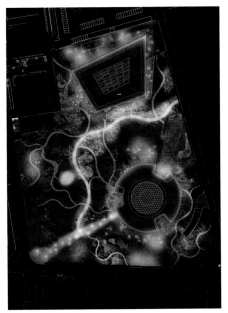

Lighting plan

©Torben Petersen & SLA Architects

©Torben Petersen & SLA Architects

Inside some of the biotopes,
various Gobo light projections were installed.

조명 또한 공원에서 중요한 역할을 한다. 낮에는 햇빛이 수목과 잎을 비추면서 하얗게 빛나는 콘크리트 길 위로 그림자를 드리운다. 밤이 되면, 세심하게 조합된 색채의 조명이 전체 경관을 비춤으로써 수목의 고유 색채와 바람에 의한 움직임을 돋보이게 한다. 몇몇 비오톱 안쪽에는 다양한 고보 라이트 프로젝션 (광선 차광막으로 너무 센 광량을 가려주거나 부분적으로 끊어서 그림자를 만드는 데 유용하게 사용된다)이 설치되어 변화무쌍한 달빛 같은 분위기를 연출한다. **번역** 우영선

In the evening the landscape is lit up by carefully aligned tones of white light which highlights and enhance the natural colors and movements of the vegetation.

©Torben Petersen & SLA Architects

Vanke Center

Martha Schwatz Partners

Landscape Architect MSP
(Martha Schwatz Partners)
Architect Steven Holl Architects
Client China Vanke Co,. Ltd.
Location Shenzhen, China
Area 520,000m²
Completion 2013
Photographs Terrence Zhang

Vanke Center, a mixed use building in Shenzhen by the largest real estate developer in China is as long as the Empire State Building is tall. It includes apartments, offices and a hotel, with a conference centre, spa and car park below ground level.

Martha Schwartz Partners(MSP) was appointed as landscape architect to re-envision and improve the existing landscape, and to transform it into high quality public and private spaces, both for the neighbourhood surrounding the development and private clientele.

Sections of the spa and swimming pool

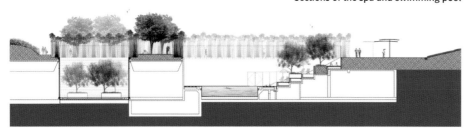

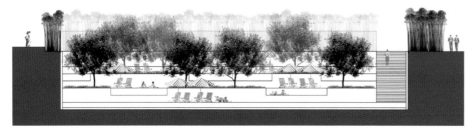

Vanke Center, a mixed use building in Shenzhen by the largest real estate developer in China is as long as the Empire State Building is tall.

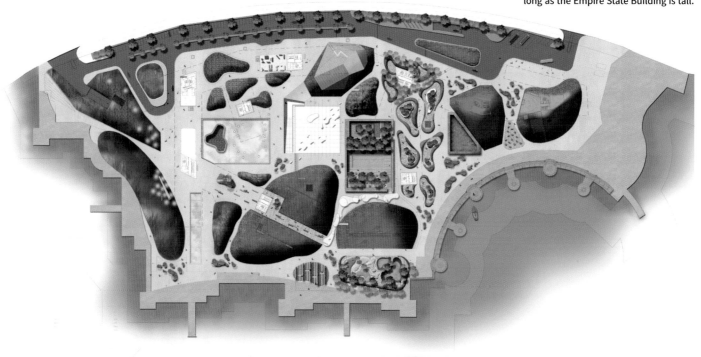

MSP transformed the existing landscape into high quality public and private spaces.

Vanke Center includes apartments, offices and a hotel, with a conference centre, spa and car park below ground level.

MSP is employing a variety of planting strategies to diversify the experience of the landscape throughout the development.

MSP came up with a concept termed "archipelago" that aimed at cleverly maintaining existing structural elements underneath the series of mounds, and employing a variety of planting strategies to diversify the experience of the landscape throughout the development.

The office zone is planted with native grasses and unified evergreen shrubs to improve the sculptural quality of the space. The hotel area was developed as a high-end landscape, with ornamental planting.

The landscape design also introduced seasonal gardens exploring temporality of landscape throughout the year, children's outdoor water play elements and a swimming pool & spa.

The office zone is planted with native grasses and unified evergreen shrubs to improve the sculptural quality of the space.

Sustainability was a key driver, particularly because of the development's LEED Platinum rating. The landscape design was developed by a series of sustainable approaches that incorporated storm water management and storage, water cleansing floating islands, native planting, habitat creation and locally manufactured and recycled materials. The development also features a state of the art urban farm for the neighbourhood. It will act as a great tool to enhance sense of community, help educate public about urban ecology and food systems and supply the grown produce to the on-site restaurant.

East hotel area

©Terrence Zhang

Planting plan shows the concept of
landscape, "archipelago."

The hotel area was developed as a high-end
landscape, with ornamental planting.

©Terrence Zhang

The landscape design was developed by a series of sustainable approaches.

반케 센터는 중국 선전에 위치한 중국 최대의 부동산 개발 기업인 차이나 반케의 본사 건물이다. 반케 센터는 미국의 엠파이어 스테이트 빌딩에 버금가는 규모로, 아파트와 업무 공간, 호텔 등으로 이루어진 주상 복합 단지다. 이 대규모 복합 단지는 특정한 기능을 수행하는 여러 개의 작은 건물들이 조합된 구조가 아닌, 하나의 거대한 건물을 35m의 고도 제한선까지 최대한 띄워 올리는 방식을 채택했다. 8개의 기둥이 건물 전체를 떠받치는 특징적인 구조와 그 아래의 굴곡진 지형은 마치 풍랑이 일다가 잔잔해진 바다 위로 거대한 건물이 떠오르는 형상을 연신시킨디.

이러한 공간 설계 방식은 바로 대상지 주변의 낮은 고도의 지역 너머로 중국 남해의 풍경을 볼 수 있는 전망을 만들어낼 수 있다는 기대감에서 비롯되었다. 또한 이는 지상 공간에 시민들을 위한 녹지를 최대한으로 제공할 수 있다는 장점으로 이어졌다. 수평적 마천루 아래로는 대규모의 정원이 조성되었으며, 거대한 공공 녹지의 하층부에는 컨퍼런스 센터와 스파 시설, 지하 주차장 등의 편의 시설이 자리 잡고 있다. 이 프로젝트는 기존 외부 공간에서 이용의 불편함을 개선하고, 주상 복합 단지가 필요로 하는 다양한 공공 및 사적 기능을 담는 것을 목표로 했다.

©Terrence Zhang

Hills viewed from urban farm

©Terrence Zhang

MSP aimed at cleverly maintaining existing structural elements underneath the series of mounds.

©Terrence Zhang

Children's outdoor play space

231

마사 슈왈츠 파트너스는 여러 개의 언덕으로 구성된 기존 경관의 구조적 요소들을 유지하면서 새로운 변화를 주기 위해 '군도'라는 설계 개념을 제안했다. 또한 전체 개발 대상지의 경관 경험을 다양하게 만들어 줄 여러 식재 전략을 채택했다. 건축물 서쪽에 해당하는 업무 구역에는 지역 자생 잔디와 상록 관목 한 종류만을 사용하여 조형적 성격을 강화했다. 그에 반해 건물 동쪽 호텔 구역은 화려한 꽃이 피는 장식적 식물을 식재해 특징 있는 경관을 만들고자 했다. 또한 그 중간에 위치한 아파트 구역에는 연간 변화하는 경관의 시간성을 경험할 수 있는 계절 정원이 조성되어 있다.

반케 센터 건물의 측면은 '선전의 창'이라 불리며 건물 아래쪽 우거진 열대 정원을 향해 360도의 전망을 제공한다. 기둥 위에 떠 있는 반케 센터의 수평적 구조는 바다와 육지에서 불어오는 바람이 공공 정원을 통해 자연스럽게 순환할 수 있도록 한다. 반케 센터의 정원에는 수영장과 다양한 크기와 형태의 언덕, 그리고 그 사이를 연결하는 보행로가 지하의 음식점과 카페 공간으로 이어진다. 밤에는 위로 떠오른 건물 아래에서 형형색색으로 빛나는 열대 식물들과 재스민 향이 한데 어우러진 공간을 산책할 수 있다.

반케 센터의 구조는 공기를 원활하게 순환시켜 주변 자연에서 조성된 미기후를 받아들이는 에너지 효율이 높다. 또한 남해에 인접한 만큼 쓰나미의 위력을 견딜 수 있도록 설계되었다. 반케 센터는 중국 남부 건물들 중 친환경 건축물 인증 제도인 LEED 평가에서 플래티넘 등급을 받은 첫 건물이기도 하다. 따라서 외부 공간 설계에서도 빗물 저류 및 관리 시스템, 수질 정화 부유섬, 자생 식물 도입, 다양한 생물 서식처 조성, 지역 내 자원 활용 및 재활용 등 지속가능성을 고려한 접근 방법을 적용했다.

The building appears as if it were once floating on a higher sea that has now subsided.

©Terrence Zhang

대상지 내에 주민들을 위한 커뮤니티 도시 농장을 조성했다. 이 농장은 공동체를 강화하고, 시민들을 위한 도시의 생태와 식품 체계에 대한 환경 교육장으로 역할 한다. 또한 반케 센터 내부 음식점에 농작물을 공급하기도 한다. 반케 센터는 열대 기후와 날씨에 최적화된, 그리고 주거 및 업무 공간에 필요한 다양한 비전을 담은 공간이다. 건축물과 외부 공간이 만들어내는 경관은 지속가능성의 여러 측면들을 수용하는 동시에 공동체를 강화할 수 있는 새로운 21세기형 주거 복합 단지로 기능할 것이다.

번역 손은신

At night, people can stroll along the archipelago of jasmine and tropical plants shining under the colorful buildings.

PWP Landscape Architecture

VMware Headquarters

Landscape Architects PWP Landscape
Architecture(Peter Walker, David Walker,
Jay Swaintek, Conard Lindgren, Nathan O.
Pepple, Eustacia Brossart, Cornelia Roppel,
Collin Jones, Steve Tycz, Mi Yang, Su-Jung
Park)
Architect From 4 Architecture
Consultants
Development Manager: Hines
Geotechnical Engineer: Rollo And Ridley
Civil Engineer: BKF
Structural Engineer: Adapture(Phase 2),
Louie International(Phase 3)
MEP Engineer: ME
Lighting: Illume
Sustainability: WSP Environment & Energy
Waterproofing: Simpson Gumpertz & Heger
Traffic: Fehr & Peers
Controls: HMA
Parking: Watry
Acoustics: Shen Milsom Wilke
Fountain Consultant: Fluidity Design
Consultants
Client VMware
Location 3401 Hillview Ave., Palo Alto, CA
94304, USA
Area 105ac
Completion 2014
Photographs PWP Landscape Architecture

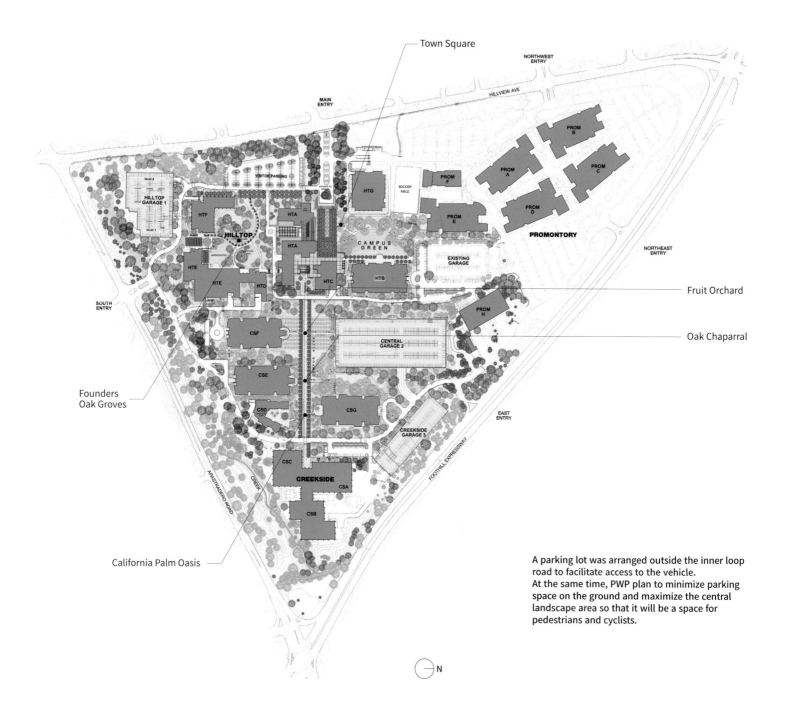

Town Square

NORTHWEST ENTRY

HILLVIEW AVE

MAIN ENTRY

VISITOR PARKING

HILLTOP GARAGE 1
level 2
level 1

HILLTOP

HTF

HTA

HTA

HTG

SOCCER FIELD

PROM F

PROM B

PROM A

PROM C

PROM D

PROM E

PROMONTORY

NORTHEAST ENTRY

HTE

HTE

HTD

HTB

HTC

CAMPUS GREEN

EXISTING GARAGE

Fruit Orchard

SOUTH ENTRY

CSF

CENTRAL GARAGE 2

PROM H

Oak Chaparral

CSE

Founders
Oak Groves

CSD

CSG

EAST ENTRY

ARASTRADERO ROAD

CREEK

CSC

CREEKSIDE

CSA

CREEKSIDE GARAGE 3

FOOTHILL EXPRESSWAY

CSB

California Palm Oasis

A parking lot was arranged outside the inner loop road to facilitate access to the vehicle.
At the same time, PWP plan to minimize parking space on the ground and maximize the central landscape area so that it will be a space for pedestrians and cyclists.

N

VMware, a leading cloud-computing software company, selected an 105 acre site in Palo Alto to become its global headquarters. Originally developed in the 1960s as the former campus for Roche Pharmaceutical, the site was dated by features typical of that era: buildings segregated by uses and acres of surface parking lots. The placement of buildings and parking lots also prioritized vehicular circulation over pedestrian walkways and human-scaled landscape spaces. PWP was hired to provide site planning and landscape architectural design services to create a new campus plan that transformed the aging site into a state-of-the-art global headquarters for the Silicon Valley company.

Water lily pond in Town Square

The fountain that sets the scenery axis of the Town Square produces a water stream of various heights.

The cherry tree, planted on the viewing terrace overlooking the outdoor lawn theater, is a tree that has been transplanted from the existing site to commemorate the old campus.

Central to the campus redesign was the goal of promoting connection and collaboration among the company's employees and expanding the architectural program to accommodate an additional 4,500 employees. To achieve this goal, PWP first studied the existing campus framework to identify potential sites for new buildings and opportunities to substitute surface parking lots for multi-level garage structures and expanded landscape spaces. The outcome of this study was a campus master plan which proposed the addition of five new buildings sited within a revised campus framework including the renovation of a few of the modernist Roche buildings. Three large parking structures were also sited adjacent to the existing perimeter loop road, providing convenient access while creating a campus core that prioritized pedestrian and bicycle access over cars.

The placement of the new buildings and the reduction in surface parking lots allowed the team to develop the new campus framework around a series of "campus quads," similar to the framework of nearby Stanford University. PWP conducted detailed design for each quad, creating a memorable and distinct landscape character for each precinct. The Promontory district comprises the group of founding VMware campus buildings built ten years before on the original 40 acres. Two new campus precincts were placed on 64 acres of newly acquired land: the Hilltop district has become the new town center of the campus with a natural amphitheater designed to hold up to 6,000 people.

From there, a turn down the hill to the Creekside District connects the bulk of the new office buildings with the new allée fountain, a seven-hundred foot long cascading water feature set within an allée of sycamore trees. The water feature forms a primary axis within the campus while also supporting connections from other campus centers. The water feature is divided into four segments by pathways that bring pedestrians to and from the campus allée. While the fountain is divided at the surface, it is hydraulically connected for its entire length by underground pipes and relies solely on gravity for the cascading downward flow, thereby minimizing its electrical and pumping requirements. Water cascades over adjustable quarter-inch stainless steel weirs and flows through a series of 67 concrete basins lined with river rock. The top of the concrete basin walls parallel the gentle slope of the adjacent pedestrian walkway.

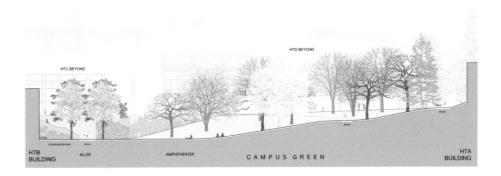

Section of Campus Green, including outdoor lawn plaza

Campus Green overlooking from entrance plaza. It was designed to be able to plan a variety of large-scale outdoor events utilizing the existing ground terrain. The opening ceremony for the completion was held at the outdoor lawn open space that can accommodate about 6,000 people.

The oak forest dedicated to commemorating the founders shows a side of the VMware campus design concept "campus in the forest."

The fountain's walls are a comfortable height and used for seating. The allée passes through three generous and iconic California landscape types, giving each of the new buildings personalized identity through their landscape context—an orchard, a live oak chaparral, and a California Palm Oasis.

PWP reconfigured the vehicular and pedestrian access to and through the campus, promoting pedestrian and bicycle circulation within the campus core. A loop perimeter road planted with additional redwood and oak trees gives the visitor experience an enhanced rural character, distributing all of the cars in a series of highly efficient parking structures, eliminating what was once an experience dominated by cars. The VMware campus is now the largest technology campus in Palo Alto and is affectionately referred to as "the campus in the forest."

Founders Oak Grove. A panoramic view of the Hilltop area planned as the visitor center of the new campus.

선도적인 클라우드 컴퓨팅 소프트웨어 회사인 VM웨어는 글로벌 본사를 위해 팔로 알토에 있는 105에이커 크기의 대상지를 마련했다. 본래 1960년대에 로체 파마세티컬의 캠퍼스로 개발되었던 대상지는 당시의 전형적 특징을 보인다.

구 캠퍼스는 용도와 지상 주차장 면적에 따라 영역이 분리되었는데, 빌딩과 주차장의 위치는 보행자를 위한 보도와 휴먼 스케일의 조경 공간을 고려하기보다는 차량 순환을 우선했다. PWP는 노후한 대상지를 실리콘 밸리의 최첨단 글로벌 본사로 탈바꿈시키는 새로운 캠퍼스 계획을 위해 대상지 계획과 조경 디자인을 맡았다.

Terrain analysis

Elevation

Campus landscape axis section. The eastern and western axis of the central part of the site, which leads from the entrance square to the Creekside, is formed as downhill terrain. The theme garden, the Fruit Garden, the California Oak Tree, and the California Palms Oasis, along the scenic spots of this terrain, reproduce California's natural landscape.

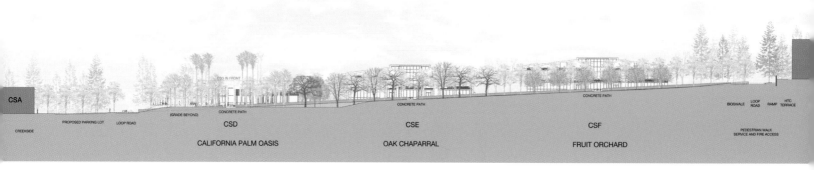

The cascade fountain is divided into four parts due to the pedestrian precinct of the campus avenue road, but the fountain system is connected all below the surface.

Approximately 6 inches of water fall lined rhizome trees meet and harmonize with sight and hearing.

캠퍼스 재조성의 핵심 목표는 회사 직원 간의 연결과 협업을 증진하고 4,500명 직원들을 추가로 수용하기 위해 건축 프로그램을 확장하는 데 있었다. 이에 기존 캠퍼스의 체계를 분석하여, 야외 지상 주차장을 다층식 주차장으로 대체하면서 조경 면적을 확보하는 전략을 세우고, 신규 건물을 지을 수 있는 부지를 물색했다. 그 결과 모던하게 지어진 로체 사의 건물 몇 동은 개조하고, 다섯 채의 새로운 건물을 추가하는 캠퍼스 마스터플랜을 제안했다. 세 개의 대형 주차 구조물은 기존의 내부 순환도로에 인접하여 위치하며, 자동차보다는 보행자와 자전거를 배려한 캠퍼스 중심부를 만들어 방문객이 편리하게 접근할 수 있도록 했다.

새 건물이 배치되고 지상 주차장 면적이 감소되면서, 인근 스탠퍼드 대학교와 비슷하게 일련의 '캠퍼스 구역'으로 전체 캠퍼스의 체계가 잡혔다. PWP는 크게 네 개의 캠퍼스 구역(곶 구역, 힐탑 구역, 센트럴 구역, 크리크사이드 구역)에 인상적이고 독특한 조경적 특징을 부여하는 섬세한 디자인 작업을 수행했다. 40에이커 크기의 곶 구역은 10여 년 전 VM웨어 캠퍼스 초기 조성 시 건축된 건물군이다. 두 개의 새로운 캠퍼스 구역이 대상지 계획을 통해 새로 확보한 64에이커 크기의 부지에 배치되었다. 힐탑 구역은 6,000명의 사람들을 수용할 수 있게 디자인된 원형의 야외 잔디 광장을 포함하며 캠퍼스의 새로운 중심부가 된다.

California Palm Oasis section. Palm Oasis, one of the tiny corridors connecting the new buildings along the campus boulevard, is a garden of native palm trees of California, such as Washington coconut, *Chamaerops humilis* and date palm.

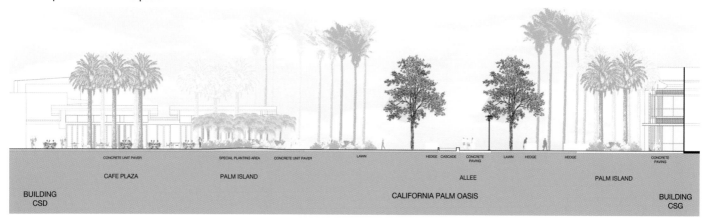

California Palm Oasis is one of the three theme gardens.
People will enter the indoor-outdoor café of the new building group while enjoying each theme garden.

힐탑 구역으로부터 크리크사이드로 내려오는 센트럴 구역에서는 신규 오피스 건물들과 700피트 길이의 캐스케이드가 있는 버즘나무 가로수 길이 연결된다. 캐스케이드는 캠퍼스 내의 주요 축을 형성하며 다른 캠퍼스 중심부와의 연결을 돕는다. 캐스케이드는 캠퍼스 가로수 길의 보행자 소로에 의해 4개의 부분으로 나뉘어있으나, 전체는 지하의 파이프에 의해 수력학적으로 연결되어 아래로 흐르는 폭포의 흐름은 온전히 중력에 의존하도록 디자인되었다. 이 넉분에 전기·펌프 설비를 최소화할 수 있었다. 물은 조약돌로 바닥을 채운 67개의 콘크리트 수반을 통과해 약 6.35mm 두께의 스테인리스 스틸 둑 위를 계단식으로 흐른다. 콘크리트 수반 벽의 윗면은 인접한 보행자 도로의 완만한 경사와 평행을 이룬다. 분수 벽은 사람들이 편하게 앉아 쉴 수 있도록 적당한 높이로 디자인되었다. 가로수 길은 과실수 정원, 참나무 숲, 캘리포니아 야자수 오아시스 등 세 종류의 특징적인 캘리포니아 고유 경관을 가로지른다. 이러한 경관적 맥락에서 신규 건물 각각에 적절한 개성이 부여된다.

The Fruit Orchard where the plum trees were used as the main species is resurrecting the personality of the theme space with the intense color contrast in the green campus.

One of the main points of the new campus planting plan was to enable a variety of planting scenarios along the pedestrian alley.

캠퍼스 중심부에서 보행자와 자전거의 통행이 원활하도록 캠퍼스를 통과하는 자동차와 보행자의 접근 방식을 변경했다. 내부 순환 도로 주변으로는 미국삼나무와 참나무를 추가로 심어 방문객들이 전원적인 특징을 경험하도록 했다. 또한 다층식 주차 공간을 효과적으로 활용해 한때 캠퍼스 부지를 잠식하던 모든 자동차를 분산시켜 처리했다. 이제 VM웨어 캠퍼스는 팔로 알토에서 가장 큰 테크놀로지 캠퍼스가 되었으며 '숲 속의 캠퍼스'라 불리고 있다.

번역 조한결

Group HAN
MBC Sangam Headquarters

Landscape Architects Group HAN
Architects Heerim Architects & Planners
Co., Ltd.
Construction Hyundai Development
Company
Client MBC
Location Seoul, Korea
Area 34,270m²
Completion 2013
Photographs Cheong-O Yu

Window Open to the World, Embracing the Nature

Located on Digital Media City(DMC) in Seoul, the new headquarters building for Munhwa Broadcasting Corporation(MBC) was designed to be open to the surrounding environment with a motive of "a window open to the world." Digital Media Street, a pedestrian-only pathway crosses the headquarters building, which lays a foundation for designing and developing the space connecting the inside and the outside, helping the architecture to function as Urban Entertainment Center.

Being a part of the grand development project for the New Millennium New Town, DMC is an advanced digital media cluster, in which media and entertainment industries such as TV, films, animations, games, music, and digital education develop technologies involved, or produce and distribute a variety of digital contents. Sangam-dong, where DMC is located, is not only a business district, but also an attractive place in the midst of a big city, where you can enjoy such natural elements as pleasant breeze from the Han River, the forest in Pyeonghwa Park, Mt. Maebongsan, Mt. Bongsan, and Mt. Bookhansan, which is a bit distant from the site.

Located on DMC in Seoul, the new headquarters building for MBC was designed to be open to the surrounding environment with a motive of "a window open to the world."

©Cheong-O Yu

Administration Center entrance plaza

The design of the landscape architecture for the new headquarters building, which embraces both cutting-edge technologies and richness of the nature, was centered around humans, the users of the architecture, and aimed at representing the analog sentiment in which one can feel and discover sensitive power of the nature by experiencing natural features like bamboo forest where the wind blows.

In addition to enhancing the symbolic image of the building as a landmark of the DMC broadcasting cluster which serves as a center of the Korean Wave and popular culture, the landscape architecture planning was developed to create different themes for every separate space including retail stores for visitors, outdoor space, and the rooftop space for the friendly office environment.

A complex of MBC buildings is composed of the space for comprehensive broadcasting management, radio studios, "Administration Center" equipped with Data Center, Production Studios, News Center, retail facilities, "Broadcasting Center" with MBC Lounge, "Media Center" made of broadcasting and communications equipment and multi-functional Open Hall. In addition, around the outdoor studio are located independent retail stores, which are reminiscent of Cloud Gate in Chicago.

Open Space Full of Culture

The main circulation planning focuses on integrating each separate building together, closely connecting Experience Studio, Open Studio, Star Park, MBC Lounge, MBC Gallery, multi-functional Open Hall, Open Stage, retail stores, and Media Plaza, and thereby forming a loop-shaped human flow. A variety of pavement patterns are introduced to create perceived differences for each space, and a group of pine trees are planted to symbolize the spirit of the public broadcasting, developing the framework for landscape architecture. In addition, the green space adjacent to the headquarters building is characterized by its bamboo trees, which contribute to creating a distinctive atmosphere among other buildings and increasing freshness

Water feature of Star Park

Star Park was planned as a street symbolizing
MBC cultural contents.

of the environment. Each space is well developed with water features, resting facilities, and a garden with small and delicate items, attracting visitors and highlighting the image as an open building.

Star Park is a street serving both as a main entrance to the MBC buildings and as a starting point for the flow of human traffic, representing the cultural contents of the broadcasting corporation appealing to the global audience. Around Experience Studio and Open Studio are small gardens and public open spaces, which provide more open space for visitors and audience, and resting space is created by planting pine trees and large zelkova trees and constructing water features and seating walls. Square M-Communication, a large-scale symbolic sculpture, represents the encounter and communication between the world and humans through the frame of vision. The planting pattern alternating bamboo and Japanese yew, along with the simple landscape made of glass, expresses the subtleness of the nature.

MBC Lounge is an open space located between Administration Center and Broadcasting Center. The design focuses on the sunlight passing through the glass walls of the building, with the facade planted with trees and equipped with water screens. The recorded sound of birds, constantly being played in the building, makes visitors feel as if they were walking in the forest. A stadium seating can work as a resting space for building tour participants.

It made the frame of the landscape with the pine tree symbolizing the spirit of the public broadcasting.

©Cheong-O Yu

Korean stars' hand print
on the street of Korean wave star

Open Stage near the streamlined shopping
facilities is a venue for small events and
a variety of purposes. It can also function
as a resting space in connection with
Digital Media Street. The front yards of the
MBC buildings in Yeoeuido and Ilsan are
relatively small, lacking the flexibility to
adjust the space according to various uses.
Broadcasting companies usually continue to
build and demolish production sets suitable
for each TV and radio program, which is
also true of their outdoor spaces being
easily changeable and adjustable. Therefore,
the outdoor space on the ground level is
designed to serve as an open plaza that can
be used flexibly for diverse programming
and different times of the day.

Open Stage near the streamlined shopping
facilities is a venue for small events and a variety
of purposes.

Healing Space for Every Taste

The New Headquarters Building opens its front garden to visitors, and provide a friendly working environment for the employees by constructing five rooftop gardens and four sunken gardens on various spots of the headquarters complex, which will serve as healing and resting spaces for those working at the buildings.

On the 4th floor of each building is a linear rooftop space for taking a walk and having a rest. On the 9th floor of Broadcasting Center is a large square which can be used both as an open studio and as a nature-inspired open space with a theme of forest. The 13th floor, used mostly by senior management, is planned as a viewing point and an outdoor living room, having Mt. Bongsan and Mt. Bookhansan as distant landscape.

The 4th floors of Administration Center and Media Center are designed to help relieve the stress of the employees working mainly for producing TV or radio programs. A carefully constructed garden space is characterized by its natural curves corresponding to the surrounding buildings and environment. An air-conditioned wooden conference room and other design features are placed to facilitate the communications for producing creative contents.

The 4th floor of Broadcasting Center is created as a cafe with outdoor tables closely related with retail facilities as it is considered a part of the vertical tour route.

Open Stage can also function as a resting space in connection with Digital Media Street.

The 9th floor of Broadcasting Center is the largest open space in the complex, and thus created as a place with a motive of forest. Walking and relaxing is one of the main purposes of this circular path, and sculptural pergolas are installed here. The open space creating the atmosphere of forest can also serve as an outdoor studio. Originally the skylight in the middle of the rooftop was regarded as a negative aspect of the space programming, but it was wisely taken advantage of by constructing bamboo forest and healing trails in harmony with the subtle lights stretching into the night sky, providing visitor with an opportunity to experience the sensitiveness of the nature.

The 11th floor of Administration Center is primarily filled with activities such as small group gatherings, providing a resting space for female employees. It also offers an amazing view of the remote mountains. Water features, sculptural benches, round tables, and seating walls are among the key elements of this relaxing and refreshing space called the Sky Garden.

Translation Ho-Kyoon Ahn

Rooftop garden on the 11th floor of the Administration Center

©Cheong-O Yu

259

세계로 열린 창, 자연의 감성을 담다

디지털미디어시티(이하 DMC) 내에 위치한 MBC 상암 신사옥은 여의도와 일산으로 이원화되어 있던 MBC를 통합하는 새로운 터전이다. 신사옥은 '세계로 열린 창'을 모티브로 하여 외부로 열린 형태로 설계되었다. 보행자전용도로(디지털 미디어 스트리트)가 MBC 신사옥을 십자형으로 가로지르는데, 외부 공간을 이와 연계하여 계획함으로써 도심형의 복합 엔터테인먼트 센터로서 역할을 하도록 했다.

DMC는 상암 새천년 신도시 개발을 목표로 방송, 영화, 애니메이션, 게임, 음악, 디지털 교육 등 미디어 산업 및 엔터테인먼트 관련 기술을 연구 개발하거나 디지털 콘텐츠를 제작·유통하는 첨단 디지털 미디어 엔터테인먼트 클러스터다. DMC가 위치한 상암동은 업무 중심 지구이기도 하지만, 한강의 강바람, 하늘공원의 억새, 평화의공원의 숲, 매봉산, 봉산, 멀리 북한산에 이르기까지 서울에서 보기 드물게 풍성한 자연 요소와 접할 수 있는 명소이기도 하다.

최첨단과 풍부한 자연의 상충된 이미지를 공유하는 MBC 신사옥의 조경은 인간, 곧 사용자 중심으로 계획하고, 최첨단 디지털을 향유하는 인간이 섬세한 자연의 힘(바람에 흔들리는 대나무숲 등)을 발견하는 아날로그적 감성을 담고자 했다.

Rooftop garden on the 9th floor of the Broadcasting Center

Resting facilities on the 9th floor of the Broadcasting Center

한류 열풍과 문화의 중심인 DMC 방송센터의 랜드마크로서의 상징성을 살리고, 방문객을 위한 판매 공간과 야외 공간, 쾌적한 근무 환경 제공을 위한 옥상 공간으로 구분되는 공간의 층위별로 각기 다른 테마를 적용하는 조경 계획을 수립했다.

MBC 건물군은 방송 전반의 업무를 수행하는 공간과 라디오 스튜디오, 데이터 센터를 배치한 '경영센터', 제작 스튜디오, 보도국, 판매 시설, MBC라운지(아트리움)가 있는 '방송센터', 방송 통신 시설 및 다목적 공개홀로 구성된 '미디어센터'가 있으며, 야외 스튜디오를 중심으로 시카고의 클라우드 게이트를 연상시키는 독립 판매 시설이 자리 잡고 있다.

문화를 품은 열린 공간

대지의 주 동선 계획은 기능적으로 분리된 건물의 배치를 하나로 엮기 위해 건물의 내외를 환상형 투어 동선으로 연결했다. 심리적인 분리를 위한 포장 패턴의 도입과 공영 방송의 정신을 강조하는 소나무 군식으로 경관의 틀을 만들고, 사옥과 인접한 녹지 지역은 DMC 내의 여타 건물과 차별성을 두고 청량감을 더하기 위해 대나무를 대표 수종으로 선정해 군식했다. 각 공간은 수경 시설과 휴게 시설 그리고 아기자기한 소품을 활용한 정원을 조성하고, 방문객이 모이는 장소로 활용하게 해 열린 사옥의 이미지를 강조했다.

스타파크는 MBC의 주 진입 공간이자 투어 동선의 시작 지점으로, 세계로 뻗어나가는 MBC 문화 콘텐츠를 상징하는 거리로 계획했다. 체험스튜디오와 보이는 라디오를 진행하는 오픈스튜디오 주변은 소규모 정원과 공개공

©Cheong-O Yu

지로 설정해 좀 더 많은 시청자와 청취자를 위한 열린 공간으로 만들었고, 소나무 군식과 느티나무 대형목, 수경 시설, 앉음벽을 중심으로 휴게 공간을 조성했다. 이곳에 설치된 미디어를 상징하는 거대한 상징 조형물은 사각의 틀을 통해 인간과 세계의 만남과 소통을 표현한다. 대나무와 주목을 활용하는 반복적 식재 패턴은 단순한 형태의 유리 배경과 어우러져 섬세한 자연을 표현한다.

MBC라운지는 건물 내의 경영센터와 방송센터 사이의 열린 공간이다. 유리 마감으로 된 외벽을 통해 들어오는 빛을 고려한 계획으로 입면을 녹화하고 워터스크린을 설치했다. 이는 스튜디오의 배경이 되고 실내 미기후 조절 장치로 활용된다. 여기에 녹음된 새소리가 흘러나와 마치 숲 속에 온 듯한 기분을 느낄 수 있도록 하고, 스탠드는 투어를 위한 중간 쉼터로 활용할 수 있다.

유선형 판매 시설 주변의 오픈스테이지는 소규모 이벤트를 위한 무대이자 상가와 인접한 행태를 수용하는 모임 공간이다. 디지털 미디어 스트리트와 연계해 쉼터로 활용 가능하다.

필요에 따라 세트를 설치하고 철거하는 방송국의 특성은 외부 공간에도 적용되는데, 이를 위해서는 가변형의 공간이 필요하다. 따라서 1층의 외부 공간은 유연한 공간 대응을 위한 광장으로 비워 시간이나 이용도에 따라 다양한 활용이 가능하도록 설계했다.

취향대로 즐기는 치유 공간

앞마당을 방문객에게 내어준 신사옥은 쾌적한 근무 환경 제공을 위해 방송센터 4층과 9층, 경영센터 4층과 11층, 미디어센터 4층에 총 5개의 옥상정원과 4개의 선큰가든을 설치하고, 직원들의 휴식과 치유를 위한 공간으로 계획했다.

각 센터 4층의 옥상은 선형으로 이루어진 공간 특성을 감안해 산책과 가벼운 휴식 공간으로 조성했다. 사각형의 넓은 오픈스페이스를 제공하는 9층은 방송센터의 야외 스튜디오이자 숲을 모티브로 자연의 감성을 담는 공간으로, 경영자가 이용하는 13층은 봉산과 멀리 북한산까지 차경이 가능한 전망 공간이자 외부 거실 개념으로 계획했다. 옥상정원을 세부적으로 살펴보면, 경영센터와 미디어센터 4층은 프로그램 제작실 위주의 공간임을 감안해 업무 스트레스를 해소하는 데 초점을 맞추었다. MBC 내외부로 트인 조망과 마주보는 건물 특성을 고려해 서로 대응하는 자연 곡선의 오밀조밀한 정원을 조성했다. 또한 냉난방이 가능한 목재 회의실과 토털 디자인 시설물을 배치해 창의적인 콘텐츠 생산을 위한 커뮤니케이션 공간으로 활용할 수 있게 했다.

방송센터 4층은 수직적 투어 동선의 일부로 인식하고, 판매 시설과 연계성을 고려해 야외 테이블 위주의 카페로 조성했다.

방송센터 9층은 가장 넓은 오픈스페이스임을 감안해 숲을 모티브로 조성했다. 소나무숲을 거닐며 치유하는 순환형 동선을 계획하고 조형 퍼걸러를 설치했다. 숲을 배경으로 하는 오픈스페이스를 확보함으로써 야외 스튜디오로도 활용이 가능하다. 공간 구성의 네거티브 요소였던 옥상 중앙의 천창은 야간에 새어나오는 빛을 배경으로 자연의 미세한 흔들림을 체험할 수 있는 대나무숲과 힐링산책로를 조성해 주야간의 활용도를 높였다.

경영센터 11층은 여사원 휴게실 등 소규모 모임 위주의 행태가 발생하고, 천장 역할을 하는 연결 브리지 하부에 위치해 자연스럽게 남북 방향으로 DMC와 봉산, 북한산을 감상할 수 있는 전망 공간으로 활용된다. 청량감을 높여주는 수경 시설을 중심으로 조형 벤치, 원형 테이블, 앉음벽 등의 휴게 시설을 배치해 편안한 휴식이 가능한 하늘정원으로 계획했다.

Night view around a streamlined sales facility

South Cape Owners Club, Clubhouse & Hotel

Seoahn Total Landscape Architecture + Design Studio loci

Landscape Architects Seoahn Total
Landscape Architecture(Young-Sun Jung),
Design Studio Loci(Seung-Jin Park)
Architects
Clubhounse: Mass Studies(Min-Suk Cho)
Hotel: BCHO Architects Associates
(Byoung-Soo Cho)
Landscape Supervision Mi-Yeon Kim
Landscpae Construction Daesan
Landscape Architecture(Eun-Gui Lee)
Location Namhae, Korea
Area 33,000m²
Completion 2013
Photographs Cheong-O Yu

Early stages sketch

Final plan. Amount of water decreased
in comparison to the initial plan,
yet the bedrock area increased considerably.

1. Clubhouse
2. Linear Suite (Hotel)
3. Open Green
4. Rock Garden
5. Hotel Garden
6. Event Green
7. Mounding Green
8. Putting Green
9. Outdoor Pool
10. Parking Lot

The term, "Namhae(south sea)," always brings out certain expectation from us. Any urban dweller can easily imagine an ocean that is far-out enough that one must run for quite some time, clean, blue water and scorching sun, and smooth leaves of sylvan evergreen broadleaf trees. It is where one jumps into the clear ocean water without hesitation, a place opposite of irritating and hostile scenery of the city. South Cape Owners Club is at the height of this southern sea.

South Cape Owners Club is located on the protruding area on the eastern side of Changseondo Island, allowing one to view the ocean from all sides.

The building has a continuous flow in the form of a low crawling on the ground.

267

It was the midsummer of 2012 when our team decided to pursue this project and paid a visit to the site. After five hour drive, we arrived not at the imagined southern seashore but at a large construction site. Although 18 hole golf course was finished as it was in a state of pseudo-operation, the clubhouse and the hotel vicinity(our design site) was simply a construction site covered by clouds of dust. As the completion date was still a year away, one can imagine the kind of condition we encountered at the site. Landscape architecture design usually finds its clue by visiting and studying the site prior to the construction phase; as this was a case where construction had already undergone its way, the usual clue-search could not take place. We were stumped.

The central space of the Club House is attracting the scenery of the exciting scale because the boundary between the inside and outside is vague.

Despite the conditions, however, the ocean view from the clubhouse or the hotel building was incredible. As the site was located on the protruding area of the island, topographically speaking, it had access to an open view of the ocean on all sides. Architectural plan was prepared while taking such scenic views into consideration. Even for space or landscape device formed by landscape architecture, concerns over such scenery is of foremost significance and a starting point. How to realize this idea, then, becomes the pivotal point of the design.

There was a steep slope between buildings.
On this slope, natural ground cover flowers were planted.

Buildings are constructed near the ground level, as if crawling; they form a continuous flow rather than conveying angular, independent mass. Outer cover painted bright grey, color that best reflects the southern sunlight.

Most users at golf resorts use automobiles or electronic gold carts. They can enjoy the ocean from all sides, and the scenery is stirring. The space created by the golf course is incomparable to urban parks or gardens in terms of its expansive scale. Buildings are constructed near the ground level, as if crawling; they form a continuous flow rather than conveying angular, independent mass. Outer cover painted bright grey, color that best reflects the southern sunlight. As we were trying to build the residence closer to the view, steep inclines were created; while considering the adequate size of the parking lot that will satisfy the regulations, we realized that the large parking space had to be built on a spot with the best views. Ocean breeze, which provides refreshing air for the most part, may sometimes uproot trees and plants with unimaginable speed. Salinity from ocean breeze may cause some trees to wither away.

Around the putting green

There is no need for a carnival of peculiar plants against the beautiful oceanscape. One needs simply to accept the atmosphere of the blowing winds and perhaps add scent to such breeze.

For most cases, the best design method is to find the simplest solution. There is no need for a carnival of peculiar plants against the beautiful oceanscape. One needs simply to accept the atmosphere of the blowing winds and perhaps add scent to such breeze. When leaves fall and delicate branches become exposed in the autumn, to be able to feel the winter sea between the branches is good enough. If during the midsummer, sylvan grass, tall as a child, can make the sounds of bustling grass against winter breeze, it should be good enough, as well. As one should expect a blossoming in spring, blue flowers—like the color of the ocean—can begin to bloom in spring. Two to three kinds of arbores including the nettle tree, few types of silver grasses such as blady grass, and flowering plants that bloom in blue, as well as rosemary. Planting list is very simple. But to control the position and the dynamics of the plant materials is a difficult process. At the same time, it is the designer's job to determine how the atmosphere among the materials will balance, and to configure the relationships of the times between blossoming and falling of the flowers. If the effort one puts into the design of the iconography is 1, configuration on site requires ten times of such effort.

Panoramic landscape from inside the clubhouse

Large bedrock surfaced during soil preparation for the clubhouse and hotel building constructions. We had initially considered removing the bedrock, but decided to refine and incorporate it into the garden after several consultations. As the stone was brittle and had high iron content, which had caused discoloration, bedrock itself had a unique beauty to itself; we therefore decided to clean it up and use as part of the landscape architecture. One of the solutions was to add a water bowl to the bedrock. bowl is suspended above the ground in tranquility, reflecting the grotesque bedrock surface onto the edge of the water. Water flows along the thin metal plate, overflows out to a stream via waterways. Large and small rocks, chipped off from the bedrock, are placed in vicinity to the waterways. This is the section of the garden that is encircled by the low-rise hotel buildings.

Clubhouse and the hotel building areas at the South Cape Owners Club were designed with completely different concept from the golf course. Wind, illumination, shadows, and scent are the most important keywords that explain the design. Focus was given to making sure the jewellike individual qualities of each plant comes through even in a collective setting. Perhaps all these were luck, bestowed upon us from the "southern ocean." **Translation** Ho-Kyoon Ahn

If during the midsummer, sylvan grass, tall as a child, can make the sounds of bustling grass against winter breeze, it should be good enough, as well.

남해南海라는 말은 늘 어떤 기대감을 가지게 한다. 서울이나 그 언저리에 둥지를 튼 사람이라면 한참을 달려가야 하는 멀리 있는 바다를 떠올리고, 그만큼 맑고 청정한 바다와 작렬하는 태양, 짙푸른 상록 활엽수의 반질반질한 이파리들을 쉽게 연상한다. 도시의 짜증나고 살벌한 풍경과는 정반대의 지점에 있으므로, 남해는 마땅히 무작정 달려가서 투명한 바닷물에 온몸을 내던져야 하는 그런 곳이다. 사우스케이프 오너스 클럽은 적어도 위치적으로 그 남해 바다의 정점에 있다. 그냥 막연한 남해 바다가 아니라, 행정구역상으로도 남해군에 속한다.

우리 팀이 이 프로젝트를 수행하기로 결정하고 현장을 방문한 것은 2012년 한여름이다. 차로 무려 다섯 시간을 달려 도착한 현장은, 우리가 꿈꿔왔던 남해가 아니라 그냥 거대한 공사장이었다. 18홀의 골프 코스는 이미 가운영 상태였으므로 제대로 된 모습을 갖추고 있었지만, 정작 우리가 설계를 진행할 클럽하우스와 호텔동 주변은 흙먼지가 날리는 공사 현장일 뿐이었다. 아직 준공을 일 년여 남기고 있었으니 현장 상태가 어떠했는지는 미루어 짐작할 수 있을 터이다. 조경 설계란 보통은 공사 개시 이전에 현장을 보면서 설계의 실마리를 찾는 것인데, 이번 경우는 공사가 한참 진행된 상태이다 보니, 그럴 여유가 없었다. 참 난감한 일이다.

Hotel buildings from rock garden

그럼에도 불구하고 클럽하우스나 호텔동에서 바라다보는 바다 조망은 최상이었다. 지형적으로 섬의 돌출된 부분에 있었기 때문에 대체로 사방으로 개방된 바다 조망을 확보하고 있었다. 건축 계획 역시 이러한 조망을 최우선으로 고려해서 만들어진 것이다. 당연한 논리겠지만 조경에서 만드는 공간이나 경관적인 장치 역시 이 조망에 대한 배려가 가장 중요한 출발점이 된다. 그런데 그것을 어떻게 구현하는지가 설계의 관건이 되는 것이다.

우선은 공간의 스케일을 이해하고 점검해 보는 것이다. 골프리조트의 경우 이용자들의 대부분은 자동차나 전동카트를 이용한다. 거의 사방으로 바다를 즐길 수 있으며 그 조망은 장쾌한 스케일이다. 골프 코스가 만들어내는 공간의 스케일 역시 도시 공원이나 정원과는 차원이 다른 빅 스케일이다. 건축물은 지면에 낮게 포복하는 형태인데, 각지고 독립적인 매스를 가지기 보다는 연속적으로 이어지는 흐름을 가진다. 외피는 남해의 태양빛을 가장 잘 반사하게 하는 밝은 회색 톤이다. 조망에 좀 더 접근해서 집을 지으려다 보니 만만치 않은 급경사면이 발생하고 있었고, 규정을 만족하는 주차장 규모를 따지다 보니 가장 좋은 지점에 대형 주차장이 만들어져야 하는 문제도 발생한 것이다. 바다로부터 불어오는 바람은 대체로 기분 좋은 선선함을 제공하지만, 때로는 무시무시한 속도로 나무들을 뽑아버리기도 한다. 바람에 묻어오는 염분에 어떤 나무들은 고사할 수도 있다.

A stream in the hotel courtyard. The overflowing water is connected to the stream through the channel.

많은 경우에 가장 좋은 설계는 가장 단순한 해법을 찾는 것이다. 아름답게 펼쳐지는 바다의 풍광에 맞서서 기기묘묘한 식물들의 잔치를 벌일 필요는 없다. 바람이 불어오는 대로 그 느낌을 받아주면 되는 것이고, 그 바람에 향기를 보태줄 수 있으면 좋은 것이다. 따뜻한 기후 덕에 상록수가 많은 이 지역에서, 가을에 잎이 지고 섬세한 나뭇가지들이 잘 드러나서 그 사이사이로 겨울 바다를 느낄 수 있으면 좋은 것이다. 한여름에 씩씩하게 아이 키만큼 자라서 무성했던 풀들이 겨울바람에 사사삭 흔들리는 소리를 내는 것 역시 좋은 것이다. 그래도 이른 봄에는 꽃소식이 있어야 하니, 바다 빛을 담은 푸른 꽃들이 봄부터 계속 피어나면 되는 것이다. 팽나무를 비롯한 두 세 종류의 교목, 띠풀을 포함한 서너 종류의 억새풀들, 로즈마리에 더해 두세 종류의 푸른 꽃이 피는 초화. 식물 리스트는 지극히 단순하다. 그러나 식물 재료의 강약과 배치 조정은 상당히 까다로운 작업이다. 마찬가지로 재료들 간의 분위기가 어떻게 조화를 이룰지, 꽃피고 잎이 지는 시간의 관계를 어떻게 설정할지는 온전히 설계자의 몫이 된다. 도상圖上의 설계에 1만큼의 공력이 들었다면 현장에서의 조정에는 10만큼의 공력이 필요하다.

During the construction work between the clubhouse and the hotel, the huge rock was exposed. We trimmed it well and used it as a landscape tool.

The pool made of thin iron seems to
float still on the ground.

Large and small rocks, chipped off from the bedrock, are placed in vicinity to the waterways.
This is the section of the garden that is encircled by the low-rise hotel buildings.

279

클럽하우스와 호텔동 공사를 위해 정지 작업을 하던 중에 거대한 암반이 드러났다. 원래는 이 암반을 들어내려고 했으나, 수차례의 협의 과정 끝에 암반을 잘 다듬어서 정원의 일부로 활용하기로 했다. 석질石質이 단단하지 않아 쉽게 부서지고 철분 함유도 높아서 색이 변색되는 문제가 있었지만, 암반 자체가 가지는 독특한 매력이 있으므로 약간의 정리를 통해 조경 요소로 활용하기로 했다. 그 해법 중의 하나로 암반에 붙여서 넓은 수반을 만드는 것이다. 수반은 고요하게 지면으로부터 떠 있는 형태로 그로테스크한 암벽면을 그대로 수변에 반사시킨다. 물은 얇은 철판면을 따라 넘치고 수로를 통해 계류로 연결된다. 계류 주변에는 암반에서 부서져 내린 크고 작은 바위들이 놓여진다. 바로 이 부분은 낮은 호텔동에 의해 위요된 정원 영역이다.

사우스케이프 오너스 클럽의 클럽하우스와 호텔동 영역은 골프 코스와는 전혀 다른 개념으로 디자인되었다. 바람과 빛, 그림자, 향기가 디자인을 설명하는 가장 중요한 키워드였으며, 개별 식물들이 가지는 보석 같은 개성이 집합적인 상태에서도 잘 드러날 수 있도록 하는 것에 집중하였다. 어쩌면 이 모든 것이 '남쪽 바다'가 우리에게 준 행운인지도 모르겠다.

Wind, illumination, shadows, and scent are the most important keywords that explain the design.

Part 3.

WATERFRONT

Hargreaves Associates

Haihe Riverfront Ribbon Park

Landscape Architect Hargreaves
Associates(George Hargreaves, Alan Lewis,
Wright Yang, Joon Kim, Ji-Su Choi, Zhe
Chen)
Local Landscape Architect Tianjin Bohai
Urban Planning & Design
Civil Engineering Sherwood Design
Engineers
Fountains Dan Euser Waterarchitecture
Lighting Design OneLUX
Marine Engineering Moffat & Nichol
Client New Town Development Company,
Tanggu PRC
Location Tanggu District, Tianjin, PRC
Completion 2014
Image Hargreaves Associates
Photographs Hargreaves Associates
Aerial Photographs Tianjin Bowei
Yongcheng Technology

The Ribbon Park in the Binhai New District of Tianjin, PRC is located along the Haihe River delta less than 2 miles from the Bohai Sea. Linked through public transit and a ferry system with the new high speed rail terminus from Beijing, this emerging Binhai urban development district will become a business and tourist destination, and the park is envisioned as an open space centerpiece along the riverfront. It is organized into five distinct zones from south to north—Delta Islands, Riparian Forest and Meadow, Central Plaza, Botanical Forest and Signature Garden—that reinforce the adjacent urban development land uses with more residential in the south and more mixed use and tourist commercial in the north. As a 30 hectare, 1.5 kilometer feature for the district, the park aims to establish a new paradigm for waterfront open space design in Northern China.

The proximity to the sea however posed many challenges common to coastal park design including a high, salty water table, low land elevations with little topography, strong winds and seasonal river flooding. These natural conditions along with severely frigid winters and flooding summers, combined with the results of decades of industrial ship building and porting of coal and minerals were at odds with the future visions of a green urban riverfront park. Hence the design tackled these issues head on in the following manners—creative flood control, storm water management, improve soil quality and resuscitate waning regional ecologies—while establishing public park destinations through passive and active programming.

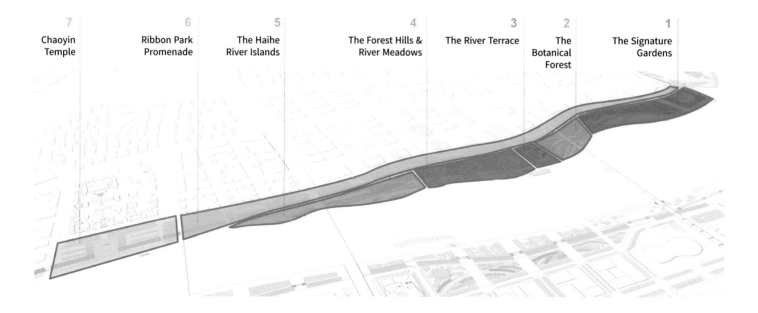

7	6	5	4	3	2	1
Chaoyin Temple	Ribbon Park Promenade	The Haihe River Islands	The Forest Hills & River Meadows	The River Terrace	The Botanical Forest	The Signature Gardens

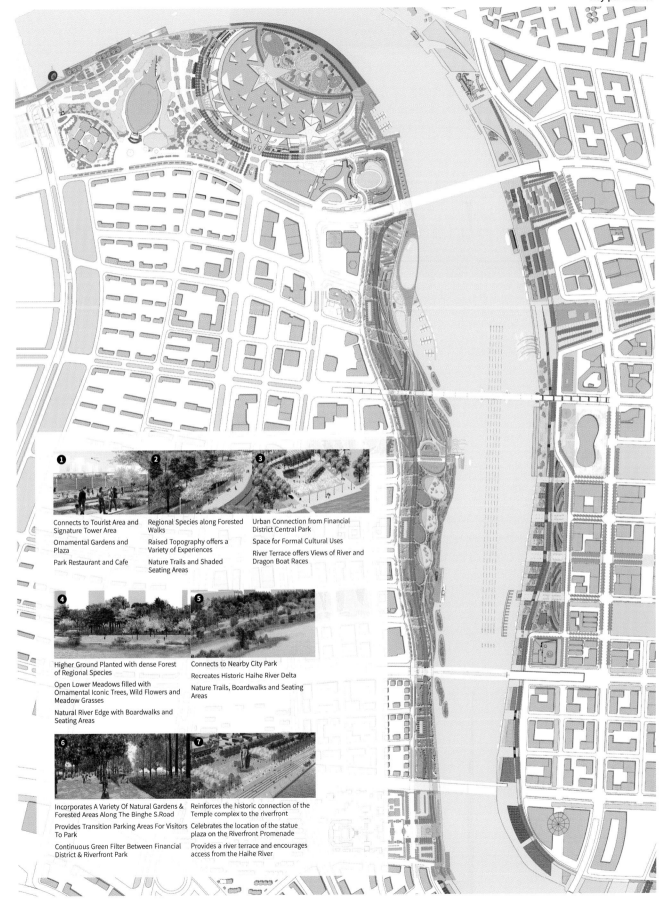

1
Connects to Tourist Area and Signature Tower Area

Ornamental Gardens and Plaza

Park Restaurant and Cafe

2
Regional Species along Forested Walks

Raised Topography offers a Variety of Experiences

Nature Trails and Shaded Seating Areas

3
Urban Connection from Financial District Central Park

Space for Formal Cultural Uses

River Terrace offers Views of River and Dragon Boat Races

4
Higher Ground Planted with dense Forest of Regional Species

Open Lower Meadows filled with Ornamental Iconic Trees, Wild Flowers and Meadow Grasses

Natural River Edge with Boardwalks and Seating Areas

5
Connects to Nearby City Park

Recreates Historic Haihe River Delta

Nature Trails, Boardwalks and Seating Areas

6
Incorporates A Variety Of Natural Gardens & Forested Areas Along The Binghe S.Road

Provides Transition Parking Areas For Visitors To Park

Continuous Green Filter Between Financial District & Riverfront Park

7
Reinforces the historic connection of the Temple complex to the riverfront

Celebrates the location of the statue plaza on the Riverfront Promenade

Provides a river terrace and encourages access from the Haihe River

To address flood control and the low elevations, the levee structure was pulled away from the water edge closer to the city and established the tree lined upper promenade that serves as the pedestrian spine of the project, and spatially, the high ground datum. From there, in the southern portion of the site in the Riparian and River Island zones, forest-filled land forms rise up and coastal grassy meadows slope down towards the river and the lower promenade. The higher ground allowed for healthier soils to nourish regional upland ecologies while the man-made topographies choreograph the storm water surges into perched cleansing wetlands that, once topped out, release into the river. These riparian wetlands offer a new, fresh water vitality along the higher natural edge while the saltwater river edge is laid back with structurally reinforced membranes that support coastal marsh plantings. Hence the two ecologies coexist with innovative topographies, soil placement, water management and plantings. Additionally, portions of the existing concrete canal were retrofitted into water storage cisterns for water reuse during dry seasons.

Upper promenade

Forest-filled land forms rise up and coastal grassy meadows slope down towards the river and the lower promenade.

288

The plaza is designed as a dynamic and flexible open space with an arced seating grove, an interactive fountain and a river terrace. It is also supported by a service pavilion with cafes, ticketing functions and ferry operations facilities.

Interim phase

Wet season 1

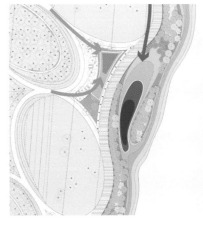

Wet season 2

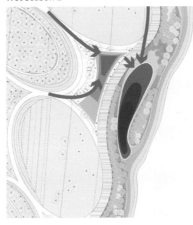

Release to river

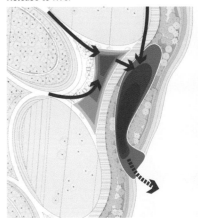

289

Directly north of this riparian zone of the project is the Central Plaza which is positioned as a cross roads between the Xiang Luo Wan central tower complex to the west and the ferry stop to the east. As a major transportation access point to and from the urban district, as well as a centerpiece plaza for programmed activities—festivals, performances, displays—the plaza is designed as a dynamic and flexible open space with an arced seating grove, an interactive fountain and a river terrace. It is also supported by a service pavilion with cafes, ticketing functions and ferry operations facilities. The cross site promenade links the urban district directly with the ferry stop and provides taxi and shuttle service access.

Further north are the more urban areas of the Botanical Forest and Signature Garden zones. There, in contrast to the Riparian Forest and River Island zones, a more structured approach is incorporated to address the shallow soil elevation and long slope from the upper promenade to the water's edge. A series of botanical "ridges" that generally parallel the river and upper promenade accomplish two things—create higher ground and redirect water laterally in 'valley paths' between ridges. This provides rich planting soils and soil depth for the botanical display and reduces runoff and erosion during storm events. As these forest ridges move north they transform into regional gardens of flowering trees and shrubs and culminate in two orchard groves. The regional species

Central Plaza which is positioned as a cross roads between the Xiang Luo Wan central tower complex to the west and the ferry stop to the east.

Central Plaza

were carefully selected; one, to ensure sustainable growth in the challenged environment, and two, based on their winter conditions, i.e. color and structural form to provide beauty even in the dormant season.

As the northern area of the project anticipates heavier pedestrian activities given the mixed use and tourist related development programs, the lower promenade expands into a broad riverfront boardwalk, or deck, that is then programed with a series of water related venues including a marina, paddle boat basin, a water garden, interactive fountains and a model boat pond that converts into an ice skating and winter ice sculpture court in the freezing months. This collection of the five park zones is unified by the upper promenade along the top of the levee that parallels the river road along the urban development edge. The zone between this tree-lined pedestrian concourse and the city street is a series of lush forested areas, parking groves and forest plazas that connect the park with the perpendicular streets and locate park facilities and cafes. This linear promenade park feature will become a park destination all its own as it will allow for people to enjoy an immediate access to green open space along the city edge. This offering will provide additional layers of experience within the rich array of environments in the Haihe Riverfront Ribbon Park that aims to create the memorable places to be enjoyed for generations to come.

중국 텐진 시 빈하이 신도시에 들어선 리본 파크는 하이허 삼각주에 위치하고 있으며, 발해 만으로 부터 약 3km 떨어진 곳에 자리잡고 있다. 대중교통과 페리, 베이징에서 출발하는 신설 고속 열차 노선 등으로 연결되는 빈하이 개발 지구는 상업 및 관광의 중심지로 새롭게 부상하고 있다. 또한 리본 파크는 강변에 위치한 공공 공간의 중심축 역할을 맡게 될 것으로 기대되고 있다. 공원은 남쪽에서 북쪽으로 이어지는 다섯 개의 개성 있는 구역으로 구성되어 있는데, 델타 아일랜드, 강변의 숲과 초지, 중앙 광장, 식물의 숲, 그리고 시그니처 가든은 인접 지역의 택지 개발을 촉진하는 역할을 동시에 맡고 있다. 남쪽 지역의 경우 주거 용도로의 개발이 활발한 반면, 북쪽 지역의 경우 복합 용도를 위한 활용이나 관광객을 대상으로 하는 상업 시설의 유치가 적극적으로 추진되고 있다. 30헥타르의 면적과 1.5km 길이에 달하는 리본 파크를 통해 중국 북부 지역 수변 공공 공간 건립의 새로운 패러다임을 제시하고자 한다.

그렇지만 바다에 인접해 있는 공원의 입지 조건으로 인해 해안 공원 디자인 시 일반적으로 등장하는 여러 가지 문제점들이 나타났는데, 염분이 높은 해수, 강력한 바람, 그리고 계절에 따른 하천 범람 등을 그 예로 들 수 있다. 혹한이 몰아치는 겨울과 홍수가 밀려오는 여름을 위시한 이와 같은 자연 조건은, 수십 년에 걸친 조선 산업 그리고 석탄 및 기타 광물의 수출입 이력이 가져다준 결과물과 어우러져, 녹색 도심 수변 공원이라는 미래 비전의 실현에 암울한 그림자를 드리웠다. 따라서 디자인 과정은 이러한 문제를 해결하는 데 초점을 맞춰 진행했다. 즉 창의적 홍수 통제, 빗물 관리, 그리고 토질 개선 및 약화된 지역 생태의 복원 등을 시행하는 한편, 능동적인 프로그램과 수동적인 프로그램을 병행 추진함으로써 공공 공원의 방향성을 수립하고자 했다.

©Tianjin Bowei Yongcheng Technology

Signature Garden

The more urban areas of the Botanical Forest and Signature Garden zones

©Tianjin Bowei Yongcheng Technology

Botanical Forest

A series of botanical "ridges" that generally parallel the river and upper promenade accomplish two things(create higher ground and redirect water laterally in "valley paths" between ridges).

홍수 통제와 저지대 문제를 해결하기 위해 도심과 가까운 수변에 위치한 제방 구조물을 이동시키는 한편, 나무를 식재한 상층부 산책로를 설치해 보행로의 뼈대를 마련했다. 이곳을 기준으로 대상지의 북쪽 지역인 강변의 숲과 리버 아일랜드 구역으로는 숲으로 가득 찬 토지가 위로 솟아오르고, 해안 초지가 강변 및 저층부 산책로를 향해 완만한 경사를 이루며 이어진다. 높은 지대에 위치한 토지에서는 건강한 토양이 마련되어 토착 고지대 생태가 번성하게 되며, 인공적으로 구성된 지형을 통해 빗물은 수질 정화용 습지로 흘러들게 되고, 이 물은 이후 강으로 흘러들어가게 된다. 이러한 강변 습지는 자연에 가깝게 변모된 물가를 따라 강에 새롭고 신선한 생명력을 불어 넣는다. 더불어 염수가 섞인 강변 지역은 구조적으로 강화된 차단막을 따라 뒤로 밀려나게 되며, 이곳에서는 해안 습지 식재도 가능하다. 이렇게 되면 두 가지 서로 다른 생태가 혁신적 지형, 토양 배치, 물 관리, 그리고 식재 등을 통해 공존할 수 있게 된다. 또한 기존의 콘크리트 수로의 일부는 물 재활용을 위한 물 저장 시설로 재배치했다.

대상지의 강변 구역 바로 북쪽으로는 중앙 광장이 있다. 이 광장의 서쪽으로는 샹루오완 센트럴 타워 콤플렉스가, 동쪽으로는 페리 터미널이 위치하고 있어 일종의 교차로 역할을 하고 있다. 축제, 공연, 전시 등 다양한 프로그램이 진행되는 중심 광장일 뿐만 아니라, 도심 지역으로의 이동이 이뤄지는 주요한 교통 거점으로서, 중앙 광장은 역동적이며 유연한 공공 공간으로 설계되었으며, 좌석 공간, 인터렉티브 분수, 그리고 강변 테라스 등의 시설을 갖추고 있다. 또한 광장에는 서비스 파빌리온을 배치해 카페, 매표소, 그리고 페리 운영 시설 등이 들어설 수 있도록 했다. 십자형 산책로를 통해 페리 정류장과 도심이 직접 연결되도록 하는 한편, 택시 및 셔틀 서비스에 대한 접근성을 확보했다.

북쪽으로 이동하면 도회적인 느낌의 공간인 식물의
숲과 시그니처 가든 구역을 만나게 된다. 강변의
숲이나 리버 아일랜드 구역과 대조적으로 체계적인
접근 방법을 차용했는데, 깊이가 얕은 토양과
상층부 산책로에서 강변까지 이어지는 길다란
경사면을 감안해야 했기 때문이다. 강 그리고 상층부
산책로와 전반적으로 평행하게 늘어선 일련의 식물
'등성이'들을 통해 두 가지 목표를 달성하고 있다.
높은 지대를 만드는 동시에 물의 흐름을 비스듬하게
바꿔놓음으로써 등성이 사이의 이른바 '계곡 수로'로
흘러들어가게 하는 것이다. 이를 통해 비옥한 식재용
토양과 토양의 깊이를 확보하는 한편, 폭우 시
지표면을 흐르는 빗물의 양과 침식을 감소시키는
효과를 거두게 된다. 숲으로 구성된 이러한 등성이는
북쪽으로 이동하면서 화목류와 관목 등으로 구성된
토착 식물 정원으로 변모한 뒤 끝으로 두 개의
과수원으로 마무리된다. 토착종들을 매우 사려 깊게
선택하여 식재하였는데, 첫째 척박한 환경 속에서
지속가능한 성장을 보장할 수 있을 것, 둘째 겨울
동안에도 색상과 모양이 충분한 아름다움을 보여줄
수 있을 것 등 몇 가지 조건을 충족시켜야만 했다.
북쪽 지역에는 더 많은 보행자가 방문할 것으로
예상되는데, 복합 활용이나 여행자를 대상으로 한
개발 프로그램이 추진되고 있기 때문이다. 저층부
산책로는 널찍한 강변 보드 워크나 데크까지
연장되고, 이는 정박지, 외륜선 계류장, 워터 가든,
인터렉티브 분수, 그리고 모형 선박 연못 등과
결합된다. 특히 모형 선박 연못은 동절기 동안
스케이트장과 얼음 조각 전시장으로 변신하게
된다. 공원 내 다섯 개의 구역은 상층부 산책로를
통해 일관성을 지닌 하나의 집합체로 통합되는데,
산책로는 도심 개발 지역의 가장자리를 따라 들어선
강변 도로와 나란히 위치한 제방의 윗부분을 따라
건립되었다. 나무가 늘어선 보행자용 콘코스와
도심지 거리 사이에 위치한 구역은 무성한 숲, 주차
공간, 그리고 숲 광장 등으로 채워지게 되는데, 이를
통해 공원과 수직적으로 구성된 거리를 하나로
연결하고, 공원 시설과 카페 등이 들어설 수 있는
공간을 확보했다. 이러한 선형 구조의 산책로형
공원은 그 자체로서 매력적인 공원이 될 수 있을
뿐만 아니라, 사람들에게 도시 외곽에서 녹색 공공
공간을 손쉽게 즐길 수 있는 기회를 마련해줄
것이다. **번역** 안호균

Thomas Balsley Associates + WEISS/MANFREDI

Hunter's Point South Waterfront Park

Park Designers Thomas Balsley Associates,
WEISS/MANFREDI
**Prime Consultant and Infrastructure
Designer** ARUP
**Ecological Systems and Restoration
Ecologist** Edesign Dynamics
Marine Engineering Halcrow
Public Art Karyn Olivier
MEPFP Engineering A.G. Consulting
Engineering, P.C.
Environmental Engineer YU & Associates
Client New York City Economic
Development Corporation
Location Long Island City, New York, USA
Park and Green Streets(Phase 1) 9.5ac
Pavilion 12,000ft²
Completion 2013
Photographs Albert Vecerka Esto, Wade
Zimmerman

Hunter's Point South Waterfront Park is phase one of a larger master plan that emcompasses the transformation of 30 acres of post-industrial waterfront on the East River in Long Island City and includes the largest affordable housing building poject in New York City since 1970's. Surrounded by water on three sides, Hunter's Point South is a new model of urban ecology and a laboratory for innovative sustainable design. The park and open space is a design collaboration between Thomas Basley Associates and WEISS/MANFREDI with ARUP as the prime consultant and infrastructure designer.

The site is waterfront and city, gateway and sanctuary, blank slate and pentimento. Design leverages the site's industrial heritage and spectacular views to establish a resilient, multi-layered recreational and cultural destination. Adjacent to a future school and an emerging residential development of 5,000 permanently affordable units, the park will provide a public front door and new open spaces for recreation that connect to the surrounding communities. The integrated design weaves together infrastructure, landscape, and architecture to transform a post-industrial waterfront site into new ecological corridors that anticioate the inevitable patterns of flooding and rising water levels along the East River, transforming Hunter's Point South into both a new cultural and ecological paradigm.

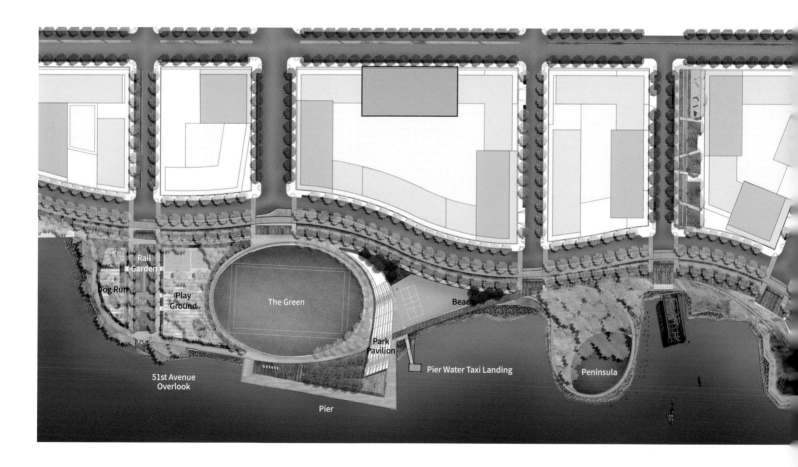

A Sustainable Waterfront

Hunter's Point South Waterfront Park has evolved from a marshy wetland to a drained landfill site and from a soft shoreline to an armored water's edge. The design incorporates numerous green initiatives, transforming a critically located but abandoned waterfront into a new urban ecological paradigm. The essence of the park is a technological and ecological system implemented to minimize non-renewable power consumption, protect and conserve water, optimize maintenance and operational practices, and create a healthy and productive environment for the community and the city.

Upland Context

Embedded in the new urban plan is a carefully conceived sustainable approach to the smart streets, bioswales, and bikeways of the new community at Hunter's Point South. Placed along the park's edge, a bioswale filters stormwater from the Center Boulevard and the upland smart streets. Each upland street enjoys the park skyline views and terminates on park vestibule entrances that have been outfited with banquette seating.

The park is based on the introduction of technology-intensive and ecological systems.

Landfill sites have been transformed from soft waterside to solid waterside.

Tree Grove

Exercise Terrace

Promontory

ation Area

Overlook

Green Oval

A new multi-use green oval defines the most generously open part of the site and offers views directly across the river to Manhattan. This green anchors the park's north precinct and is framed by a continuous path and pleated steel shade canopy on the south side which follows the curve of the oval and offers shelter for a water ferry stop and concession building.

Pathways

The path that surrounds the central green unfurls into a promenade leading to an overlook at the southern terminus of the site. This overlook, a 30-foot high cantilevered platform with views of the Manhattan skyline and the East River, is at once urbane and otherworldly, bringing the city to a precipice suspended over a new wetland water's edge. From the central promenade path, existing concrete bulk-heads are strategically replaced by new wetlands and pathways that link the major precincts and programs of the park. This path system extends to the water's edge and forms park of the "soft" edge the park. This path system extends to the water's edge and forms park of the "soft" edge infrastructure, while also providing a new landmark and destination that draws the community to the waterfront.

The pavilion offers 360-degree views of Manhattans skyline and East River.

Pavilion

The Pavilion is conceived as a continuous structure which connects the city with the water's edge. It is strategically located to support the park's active and passive recreational uses and provides a legible point if arrival and orientation. The Pavilion is divides into two buildings under one continuous canopy. It includes a maintenance and operations facility for the Department of Parks and Recreations, comfort stations, a concession building, and a raised café plaza. The Pavilion culminates at the elevated wood pier, with panoramic views of the Manhattan skyline and the East River corridor.

The folded plate shade structure recalls the maritime history of Hunter's Point and is optimized to capture storm water and solar power. Sixty-four photovoltaic panels located on the south face of the steel pleats generate 37,000 kWh per year, powering over 50% of the entire park. The design can accommodate additional panels to power 100% of the park in the future. The folded plates also collect stormwater which nourishes nearby bioswales. A richly textured brushed metal surface drapes across the outer edge of the sweep along the green sweep, and reflects the activity at the green and the general landscape.

Urban Beach

Framed by the pavilion and park path, an urban beach hosts sunning, picnicking, and beach

The folded plate-like shade structure reminds us of the maritime history of the last days of Hunter's Point, and has the optimal conditions to utilize rainwater and solar energy.

volleyball along the edge of the promenade. Here, visitors will sink their toes in the sand and take in a unique beach sunset over the Manhattan skyline.

Interpretive Rail Garden

Framed by the urban dog run and play area at the 51st Avenue vestibule, native grasses envelop freight rails to compose an interpretive rail garden narrative. A cross path weaves through to a small central plaza animated with water jets and the interation they attract.

Urban Dog Run

As a relatively new component of the 21st century urban park, the dog run has proven its long term social sustainability worth. With its distinctive water rill, stacked timber seats that recall an earlier lumberyard and animated shelter which has taken its cues from the pavilion, this dogscape has elevated the fun of dog ownership.

Play Area

Resting on a tree shaded shelf above the promenade and surrounded by native grasses, the play area promises to be the center of family activity for the park. Here at the edge of the East River an ensemble of play venues for all agees ranges from basketball and adult fitness to a children's play with lawn mound and water play channel.

헌터스 포인트 사우스 워터프런트 파크는 뉴욕 시가 추진하고 있는 원대한 마스터플랜의 제1단계 사업이라 할 수 있다. 이 계획에 따르면 롱아일랜드 이스트 강변에 위치한 30에이커 규모의 유휴 부지가 새로운 모습으로 탈바꿈하게 되며, 1970년대 이래 뉴욕 최대 규모의 중산층 대상 주택 단지 건설 사업이 추진될 예정이다. 세 면이 물로 둘러싸인 헌터스 포인트 사우스는 도시 생태계에 있어 새로운 모델을 제시하게 될 것이며, 혁신적인 지속가능한 디자인의 성패를 가늠하는 평가의 장이 될 것이다. 공원 및 공공 공간은 토마스 바슬리 어소시에이츠와 와이즈/만프레디의 협업으로 탄생하였고, ARUP이 주관 컨설팅 및 기반 시설 설계를 맡았다.

대상지는 수변 공간인 동시에 노시이고 관문의 억할을 하는 한편 보호 구역에 해당하기도 하다. 또한 아무 것도 없는 빈 공간인 듯하지만, 과거의 흔적이 어렴풋이 드러나 있다. 디자인을 통해 대상지가 가진 산업적 전통·유산과 극적인 조망을 조화시킴으로써 자체적 회복력을 지닌 다층적 구조의 여가·문화 공간을 창조하고자 하였다. 향후 인접 지역에 학교와 5,000세대의 주택 단지가 조성될 것으로 예상되고 있기에 이 공원은 소통의 장으로서 역할을 수행하는 한편, 주민들의 여가를 위한 새로운 공공 공간으로서의 기능을 담당하게 될 것이다. 통합적 디자인을 바탕으로 기반 시설, 경관 그리고 건축을 한데 어우러지게 함으로써 수변에 위치한 유휴 부지를 새로운 생태 공간으로 변모시켰다. 또한 이스트 강에서 필연적으로 나타나게 될 반복적인 홍수 및 수위 상승도 충분히 예측하여 설계에 반영했다.

Ecological wetlands constructed around the parks
cleans rainwater from the center and the smart streets.

©Wade Zimmerman

지속가능한 수변 공간

헌터스 포인트 사우스 워터프런트 파크가 들어선 부지는 축축한 습지에서 물을 뺀 쓰레기 매립지로, 부드러운 물가에서 단단한 수변으로 점차 변모해왔다. 최적의 위치를 지녔음에도 방치되고 있던 수변 공간을 다양한 환경친화적 방법으로 디자인해 새로운 도심 생태 패러다임을 보여주는 공간으로 변모시켰다. 공원의 핵심은 기술집약적이며 생태적인 시스템의 도입이다. 이를 통해 비재생 에너지원 사용을 최소화하고, 수자원의 보존 및 보전, 유지 및 관리 활동의 최적화 그리고 커뮤니티 및 도시를 위한 건전하고 생산적인 환경의 조성 등 다양한 목표를 성취할 수 있게 되었다.

고지대 환경

새로운 도시 계획을 살펴보면, 새로운 커뮤니티를 위해 헌터스 포인트 사우스에 스마트 거리, 생태 습지 그리고 자전거 도로 등을 설치함에 있어 치밀하게 구상된 지속가능한 접근 방법을 채택했음을 알 수 있다. 공원 주변을 따라 조성된 생태 습지는 중심 가로 및 고지대 스마트 거리로부터 유입되는 빗물을 정화한다. 각각의 고지대 거리에서는 공원과 도심 스카이라인이 자아내는 멋진 경치를 즐길 수 있는데, 이 거리들은 연회용 좌석 등이 마련된 공원 출입구 앞쪽까지 연결된다.

타원형 잔디 마당

다목적 타원형 잔디 마당은 대상지에서 그 개방성이 가장 뚜렷하게 드러나는 공간을 대표하고 있는데, 이곳에서는 강 건너편의 맨해튼을 조망할 수 있다. 이 녹색 공간은 공원 북쪽 구역의 중심 역할을 하고 있는데, 그 주변을 끊김 없이 이어진 산책로가 둘러싸고 있다. 남쪽으로는 주름이 잡힌 강철 캐노피가 타원의 곡선을 따라 위치함으로써 페리 정류장과 매점 건물을 이용하는 방문객들에게 그늘을 제공하고 있다.

산책로

중앙 녹지를 둘러싸고 있는 길은 공원의 남쪽 끝부분에 이르러 전망대로 연결되는 산책로로 넓게 펼쳐진다. 30피트 높이의 캔틸레버식 플랫폼인 이 전망대에서는 맨해튼의 스카이라인과 이스트 강을 조망할 수 있어 수변 공간의 낭떠러지 끝에서 도심의 숨결을 온전히 느낄 수 있게 한다. 중앙 산책로로부터 기존의 콘크리트 격벽을 습지 및 보행로를 중심으로 전략적으로 재배치함으로써 공원 내의 주요 구역을 하나로 연결할 수 있도록 하였다. 이러한 보행로 시스템은 물가로까지 이어져 이른바 '연성' 수변 기반 시설을 형성하고 있는데, 새로운 랜드마크와 볼거리를 제공함으로써 지역민들을 수변 공간으로 끌어들이는 효과를 거두고 있다.

파빌리온

파빌리온은 도시와 수변 공간을 이어주는 역할을 한다. 파빌리온의 전략적 배치를 통해 공원 내에서 벌어지는 여가 활동을 지원할 수 있도록 하는 한편, 출입과 길 찾기 등을 용이하게 해줄 확실한 이정표를 제시할 수 있도록 하였다. 파빌리온은 하나의 연속된 캐노피 아래 두 개의 개별적 건물을 두는 형태로 설계되었으며, 이곳에는 공원 행정 관리 부서를 위한 유지·운영 시설, 공중 화장실, 매점 그리고 야외 카페 등이 자리 잡고 있다. 파빌리온은 높이 세워진 나무 잔교까지 이어지는데, 맨해튼의 스카이라인과 이스트 강을 바라보는 360도 전망을 제공한다.

접혀진 판 형태의 그늘 구조물은 헌터스 포인트의 지난 시절 해양사를 연상시키며, 빗물과 태양 에너지를 활용할 수 있는 최적의 조건을 갖추고 있다. 주름이 잡힌 이 강철 구조물 위에 남쪽을 향해 설치된 64개의 광전지판은 매년 37,000kW의 전기를 생산하게 되며, 공원 전역에서 사용되는 에너지의 약 50%를 충당하게 된다. 설계에 따라 향후 광전지판을 추가로 설치하게 되면, 공원에서 사용되는 에너지 전부를 태양 에너지를 통해 공급할 수 있게 된다. 접혀진 판 구조물은 빗물을 모으는 역할도 함께 하고 있는데, 이물은 인근의 생태 습지로 흘러들어가게 된다.

도심 해변

파빌리온과 공원 보행로로 둘러싸인 도심 해변은 산책로를 따라 일광욕, 소풍, 비치 발리볼 등을 즐길 수 있는 최적의 공간이다. 이곳에서 방문객들은 맨발로 모래사장을 걸어볼 수도 있고, 맨해튼의 스카이라인 위로 펼쳐지는 멋진 일몰을 감상할 수도 있다.

레일 가든

51번가와 이어진 연결 통로 쪽에는 애견 산책로와 놀이 공간을 따라 자연초로 둘러싸인 화물 수송용 철로가 놓여있다. 철도 정원과 같은 콘셉트를 만들어내고 있는 것이다. 십자형 보행로에는 작은 중앙 광장이 마련되어 있는데, 이곳은 분수, 분수가 내뿜는 물줄기, 그리고 이를 통해 만들어지는 활기찬 에너지로 가득 차 있다.

도심 속 애견 산책로

21세기 도시 공원에 비교적 새롭게 등장한 구성 요소인 애견 산책로는 장기적으로 사회적 지속가능성에 상당한 기여를 하고 있는 것으로 알려져 있다. 독특한 실개천과 층층이 쌓아올린 통나무 의자 덕분에 방문객들은 마치 옛날 목재 집하장을 찾은 듯한 느낌을 받게 되는데, 애견 산책로 덕분에 개를 키우는 사람들은 한층 더 즐거운 시간을 보낼 수 있을 것이다.

놀이 공간

산책로 위쪽 나무 그늘 아래, 자연초에 둘러싸여 있는 놀이 공간은 공원을 찾은 가족들이 함께 어울려 즐길 수 있는 공간이다. 이스트 강의 한 귀퉁이에 자리 잡은 이 놀이 공간에는 농구장과 성인용 체련 시설에서부터 잔디 둔덕과 같은 어린이 놀이 시설까지 모든 연령대를 아우를 수 있는 다양한 시설이 조화롭게 배치되어 있다.

번역 안호균

There is a cargo transportation railroad surrounded by natural grasses on the side of the passage connecting with 51st Street, and it constitutes a "railroad garden."

©Wade Zimmerman

Nikiforidis-Cuomo Architects

New Waterfront of Thessaloniki

Design Nikiforidis-Cuomo Architects
Urban / Architectural Study Prodromos
Nikiforidis, Bernard Cuomo, Atelier R.Castro
– S.Denissof with Paraskevi Tarani, Efi
Karioti, I. Dova, E. Zografou, N. Karakosta,
N. Biskos, S. Nikolakaki, D. Pavlopoulou, F.
Valsami, E. Konstantara, N. Barkas
Structural Study Iakovos Lavasas, Maria
Stefanouri with P. Zervas, G. Nikolaidis, L.
Deda, F. Papapetrou
Electromechanical Study Dimitris Bozis,
Panagiotis Kikidis and collaborators E.P.E.,
Gerasimos Kampitsis with D. Kalofolias, D.
Iliadis, A. Fouki, F. Moshopoulou, K. Deni, A.
Savvopoulos
Phytotechnical Study Iloriki E.E. – Fotis
Fasoulas with A. Zahariadis, C. Karachristos
Geotechnical Study Evaggelos Vasilikos
with Theodosis Papaliagas
Supervision of the Studies Konstantinos
Belibasakis, Maria Zourna, Katerina Bletsa,
Eleni Fountoulidou, Sevasti Laftsidou,
Dimitris Katirtzoglou, Dimitris Sotiriadis
Supervision of the Construction Andreas
Spiliopoulos, Dimitris Tzioras, Nikolaos
Mourouzidis, Ioanna Karagianni, Spiridoula
Paraskeva
Client Municipality of Thessaloniki
Location Thessaloniki, Greece
Area 238,800m^2
Completion 2014
Photographs Aris Evdos, Bernard Cuomo,
Erieta Attali, Giorgis Gerlympos, Prodromos
Nikiforidis, Teo Karanikas, Tsoutsas

The New Waterfront of Thessaloniki is a linear place with limited depth and great length, with the characteristics of a "front," a thin layer inserted in the limit between land and sea. The project consists of a long walk along the waterfront and 13 green spaces.

In 2000, the Municipality of Thessaloniki launched an International Architectural Competition for the redevelopment of the New Waterfront of the city and in 2006 the construction of the first prize began. The New Waterfront is realized in two phases. The construction of the first part (around 75,800 m²) was completed in 2008 and the construction of the second part (around 163,000 m²) started in 2011 and ended in 2014. The total length of the New Waterfront is 3.5km.

©Bernard Cuomo

General view of the waterfront redevelopment with the Mount of Olympus in the background.

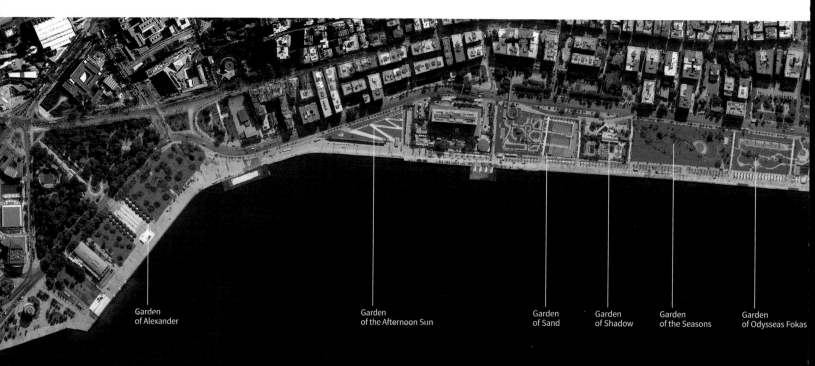

Garden of Alexander

Garden of the Afternoon Sun

Garden of Sand

Garden of Shadow

Garden of the Seasons

Garden of Odysseas Fokas

Wooden deck in the Garden of Sand

nean · Garden of the Sculpture · Garden of Sound · Garden of Roses · Garden of Memory · Garden of Water · Garden of Music

The sculpture of Georgios Zoggolopoulos

The basic purpose was the complete approach of the topic, aiming at proposed interventions that present continuity and coherence and at the same time contribute to the regeneration of the ecosystem at the borderline between sea and city. In the New Waterfront, two major characteristic areas are distinguished, which set the principles for the basic choices of the project.

The walk, right above the limit between land and sea, is an ideal place for walking, without interruptions and distractions. The paving of the coast, from the White Tower to the Concert Hall, is handled unitedly and equally, without hierarchies and alterations to its width. A cast floor is constructed along the waterfront length and all its width, wherever hard floor existed. The floor is differentiated at the ending of the breakwater towards the sea by using a wooden deck of Bangkirai.

In the inner side of the breakwater, the alternative of a shaded walk is offered. This walk with the proposed sitting-rooms among the trees, is particularly useful during the summer months as an intermediate limit-filter between the two discrete parts of the coast front: the paving and the green zone.

At the opposite side of the linear route, 13 green spaces are formed at the inner side, as a succession of "greenrooms–gardens," each with a special thematic characteristic. It's not about big "parks," but "rooms" of small size that remind of the house gardens that existed in the area and reached the natural seashore, before the landfill of the coast. The gardens are protected spaces and have their own introversion. The differentiation, the possibility of visual isolation, the shading, the surprise, the discovery or the reveal of the different, the game, the soft floors, the green: the gardens follow different ways of synthetic language, glorifying the familiar and the private, creating new collective spaces in a local scale.

The names of the gardens are successively: Garden of Alexander, Garden of the Afternoon Sun, Garden of Sand, Garden of Shadow, Garden of the Seasons, Garden of Odysseas Fokas, Garden of Mediterranean, Garden of the Sculpture, Garden of Sound, Garden of Roses, Garden of Memory, Garden of Water and Garden of Music.

Garden of the Afternoon Sun

Every part of the New Waterfront is accessible by all citizens.

©Tsoutsas

Garden of the Seasons

The main objective of the intervention was to offer the citizens a new landscape that could provide them with safe, well-planned, interesting, modern, multifunctional public spaces of high aesthetics. It was also to create a public space for all, to provide new services, alternative choices and to provoke the creation of new habits. Every part of the New Waterfront is accessible by all citizens. There has been provision for special needs and abilities, for example there are ramps, signs, playgrounds suitable for all children, a bicycle route, a special route for the blind, etc. As a result, the New Waterfront has areas with very different characteristics, which all complete a multifaceted image.

Garden of Water. At the opposite side of the linear route, 13 green spaces are formed at the inner side, as a succession of "greenrooms–gardens," each with a special thematic characteristic.

테살로니키는 그리스 북부 테살로니키 주의 항만 도시다. 테살로니키 워터프런트는 에게 해를 바라보며 아주 기다란 해변을 따라 조성된 선형의 공공 공간이다. 2000년에 이르러 테살로니키 시 당국은 기존 테살로니키 워터프런트를 새로운 모습으로 탈바꿈시키기 위한 국제 건축 공모전을 실시했다. 뉴 테살로니키 워터프런트는 총 두 단계를 거쳐 완성되었다. 첫 번째 구역(약 75,800㎡)은 2006년부터 2008년까지 3년에 걸쳐 조성되었으며, 2011년에 착공된 두 번째 구역(약 163,000㎡)은 2014년에 완성되었다. 총 면적이 238,800m²에 달하는 뉴 테살로니키 워터프런트는 바다와 육지의 경계라는 독특한 자연 및 사회문화적 생태계의 다양한 켜를 받아들여, 이를 남북으로 이어진 3.5km 길이의 산책로와 열세 곳의 녹지 공간 속에 풀어냈다.

이 프로젝트의 기본적인 목표는 바다와 도시의 경계 지역의 생태계를 되살리고 해변을 따라 연속성과 통일성을 띠는 공공 공간을 만드는 데 있다. 화이트 타워(북쪽 끝)부터 콘서트 홀(남쪽 끝)까지 이어지는 해변 길은 경사나 레벨 차이가 거의 느껴지지 않도록 처리되었다. 공간에 통일성과 일관성을 주기 위해 일정한 폭을 유지하도록 했으며, 경질 포장 처리가 필요한 모든 곳에 현장 타설 콘크리트만을 사용했다. 육지와 바다의 경계 부분(해변 길)보다 높은 레벨에 조성된 산책로는 일련의 정원을 따라 외부의 방해를 받지 않고 산책을 할 수 있는 이상적인 장소다. 해변 길과 바다의 경계에 놓인 방파제의 끝부분에는 방킬라이 소재의 목재 데크가 조성되어 있다. 산책로의 식재 공간 사이사이에는 휴게 공간이 마련되어 있으며, 이 구역은 해안가의 상이한 두 영역인 보도와 녹지 사이를 중간에서 이어주는 완충 지대 역할을 한다.

Garden of the Odysseas Fokas and the Garden of Mediterranean

©Bernard Cuomo

Interior view in the Garden of the Sculpture

Pavilion and the water tank in the Garden of the Sculpture

©Teo Karanikas

선형 가로의 해안선 반대편으로는 열세 곳의 녹지 공간이 일련의 연속적인 정원을 형성하고 있다. 모든 정원은 각기 특별한 주제에 따른 독특한 공간적 특징을 가지고 있다. 따라서 뉴 테살로니키 워터프런트는 커다란 하나의 '공원'이라기보다 다수의 작은 '방'이 연속된 것에 가까우며, 이는 해변이 현재와 같이 매립되기 이전에 시내에서 자연 해안까지 이어져 있던 주택 정원을 연상시킨다. 이 정원들은 다양한 조형 요소로 공간을 에워싸며 각각의 독립된 분위기를 더욱 고취시킨다. 나아가 차별화와 시각적 고립 가능성, 그늘, 놀람, 차이의 발견과 드러냄, 놀이, 부드러운 노면, 녹지 등 각기 다른 개념을 적용하여 차이를 두고자 했다. 그럼에도 불구하고 전체적으로는 사적이며 친밀한 공간을 조성한다는 통일된 설계 언어를 담아내고자 했으며, 지엽적인 스케일을 연속적으로 사용하여 집산적 공간을 만들어내고 있다.

이렇게 다양한 요소와 공간 조성 방식을 활용하여 시민들에게 보다 새로운 풍경을 제공하고자 했다. 시민들이 더욱 안전하고 잘 정비되고, 흥미진진하고 현대적이며, 지극히 아름다우면서도 공간 활용도가 높은 복합적 공공 공간과 독특한 경관을 체험할 수 있도록 한 것이다. 나아가 공간의 다양성은 모든 사람들이 나만의 공간을 만들어낼 수 있게 하며, 새로운 서비스와 여러 선택지를 제공함으로써 선형의 공간을 면적으로 확장시키고자 했다. 즉 워터프런트의 영향력을 인근 주택까지 더욱 확장하여 일상 속의 새로운 취미를 이끌어내는 촉매로 활용하고자 한 것이다. 뉴 테살로니키 워터프런트의 모든 공간은 시민 모두에게 개방되어 있다. 그리고 단순한 개방을 넘어 이용의 편의성을 배려한 다양한 시설—경사로와 표지판, 어린이들이 이용하기에 적당한 운동장, 자전거 길, 시각장애인용 특별 산책로 등—을 배치하여 불편함이 없도록 했다. 뉴 테살로니키 워터프런트는 다양한 공간 성격과 특징들이 모여 있는 곳이지만, 이 모든 다채로운 면들이 공존하며 조화로운 경관 이미지를 형성하고 있다. **번역** 우영선

Night in the Garden of Sound

Garden of Music

Interior view in the Garden of Roses

Topiaris

Tagus Linear Park

Landscape Architects Topiaris landscape
architecture(Luis Ribeiro, Teresa Barão,
Catarina Viana, Ana Lemos, Elsa Calhau,
João Oliveira, Rita Salgado, Sara Coelho)
Architect Atelier Difusor de Arquitectura
Client Municipality of Vila Franca de Xira
Location Póvoa de Santa Iria, Portugal
Area 15ha
International Competition 2012
Completion 2013
Photographs João Morgado

The "Fishermen's Beach" contains a set of diverse and complementary equipment primarily intended for environmental education, leisure and informal sports.

The Tagus Linear Park is an area of 15,000m² that was conquered by the surrounding communities of the industrial private sector and was felt as a democratic intervention by those forever deprived of access to the river. For the first time, people of adjacent urban communities are given recreation and leisure opportunity in direct contact with the riverside, which was until recently blocked by large industrial lots. People of all ages, from different walks of life and cultural backgrounds are now invited to come and enjoy a diverse palette of equipment and activities: from sports, fishing, walking and

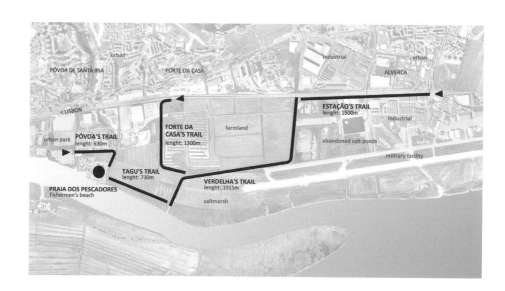

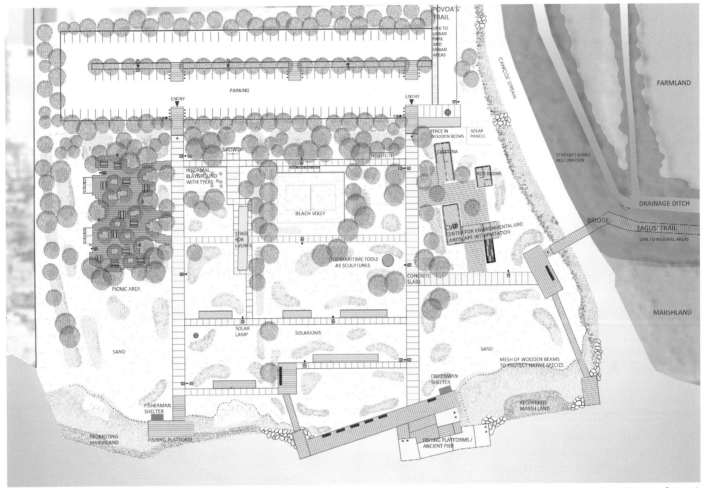

Fishermen's Beach

Sections of trails

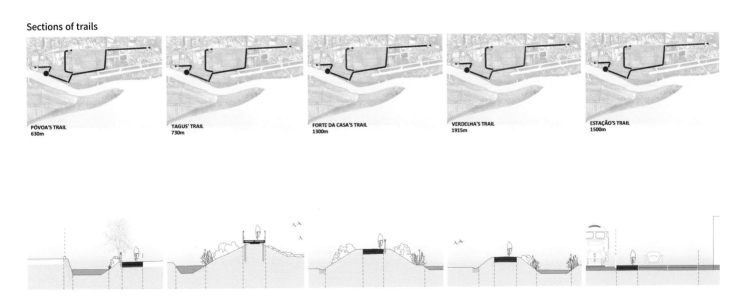

PÓVOA'S TRAIL
630m

TAGUS' TRAIL
730m

FORTE DA CASA'S TRAIL
1300m

VERDELHA'S TRAIL
1915m

ESTAÇÃO'S TRAIL
1500m

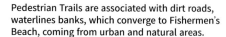

Pedestrian Trails are associated with dirt roads, waterlines banks, which converge to Fishermen's Beach, coming from urban and natural areas.

©João Morgado

cycling to environmental education, or simply to get an eyeful of the landscape. The objective was to rethink urban public space located in a complex, unexpected, almost improbable universe of urban, industrial, agricultural and natural landscape. Aiming to keep the "essence of the space" the team designed a unique greenway, grounded in the landscape's natural and cultural features, with a multitude of recreational and leisure options, safeguarding the existing natural systems and promoting the ecological regeneration of damaged areas.

The Park combines two different typologies of spaces: A single multifunctional area named "Fishermen's Beach," set by the riverside within a former sand deposit, and 6km of Pedestrian Trails associated with dirt roads, waterlines banks(streams and drainage ditches), which converge to Fishermen's Beach, coming from urban and natural areas. The connection between the 'beach' and natural areas is made through a 700m long raised wooden path by which a Bird Observatory built from old pallets can be reached.

The "Fishermen's Beach" contains a set of diverse and complementary equipment primarily intended for environmental education, leisure and informal sports: fishing platforms and shelters, picnic areas, a volleyball court, a simple playground with recycled tires, as well as platforms for sunbathing meet here in these 3ha of riverside front, to create an interesting

People of all ages, from different walks of life and cultural backgrounds are now invited to come and enjoy a diverse palette of equipment and activities.

and unique playscape. The name was inspired by the fishermen, who were sceptical at the beginning, but soon realized that the renovated space kept the "sense of place" that has attracted them to it in the past. Their constant presence has proven to be a sustainable and efficient surveillance strategy. Lighting is 100% solar.

The Centre for Environmental and Landscape Interpretation, planned for temporary exhibitions and events, is built in a modular system using recycled maritime containers. The structure is slightly raised from the ground, generating a spatial pattern that takes advantage of the views

towards the ecosystems nearby. The network of paths, made from concrete slabs, designs the main spatial structure, connecting all components. Vegetation is composed mainly of native species and was planted in clusters featuring a specific formal pattern, contrasting with the extensive sand area. The densely planted groups are protected by a mesh of individual wooden poles to help capture and secure sand, and also to protect plants from being trampled in their early stages of development.

Pedestrian Trails

대상지는 과거 민간 공단으로 둘러싸여 있었다. 이 지역 주민들은 강으로 접근하기 어려웠기 때문에 강변과 연계된 활동도 제한되었다. 타구스 리니어 파크는 이런 상황에 놓여 있던 지역 주민에게 민주적 중재물로 기능한다. 공원 조성에 따라 서로 다른 배경을 가진 각계각층의 사람들이 이곳을 찾을 것이며, 150,000m²의 광활한 대지를 따라 다양한 친수 활동이 가능해질 것이다. 타구스 리니어 파크에서는 낚시, 걷기, 사이클링, 환경 교육 또는 단순히 경관을 즐기는 등 다양한 활동이 가능하다.

대상지는 시가지와 산업 경관 그리고 농업 및 자연 경관이 혼합되어 있어 상당히 복잡한 곳이었다. 이 프로젝트의 목표는 다양한 변수가 종합된 대상지 내에 새로운 도시 공공 공간을 만들어 내는 것이다. 새로운 공원을 만들어 내기에 앞서 이곳만이 가진 '공간의 본질'을 유지하기 위해 기존의 자연 환경과 문화적 특성에 기반을 둔 독특한 그린웨이를 도입했다. 이 그린웨이는 다양한 레크리에이션 및 레저 활동의 기반이 될 뿐만 아니라, 기존 생태계를 보호하고 공업 활동으로 파괴된 환경의 재생을 촉진한다.

The Fishermen's Beach is set by the riverside within a former sand deposit.

©João Morgado

Fishermen's Beach was inspired by the fishermen.

©João Morgado

The industrial history is reflected in
the park's design.

Aiming to keep the "essence of the space" the team designed a unique greenway, grounded in the landscape's natural and cultural features.

The densely planted groups are protected by a mesh of individual wooden poles to help capture and secure sand, and also to protect plants from being trampled in their early stages of development.

타구스 리니어 파크는 크게 '낚시꾼의 해변'과 트레일로 구성되어 있다. '낚시꾼의 해변'은 강가의 모래가 퇴적되어 만들어진 땅에 조성된 다목적 공간이며, 트레일은 시가지 및 자연 지역과 '낚시꾼의 해변'을 연결하는 보행로다. 이 보행로는 대상지 내의 개울, 배수로, 둑길, 수변 제방 등을 포함하며 6km의 길이로 뻗어 있다. '낚시꾼의 해변'에서 700m의 나무 데크 길을 이용하면 자연 지역을 통과할 수 있고, 화물 운반대를 재활용하여 만든 조류 조망대까지 이어진다. '낚시꾼의 해변'은 낚시, 배구 등의 스포츠를 할 수 있는 공간이자 환경 교육장이다. 3헥타르의 면적을 아우르는 '낚시꾼의 해변'에는 낚시터와 낚시꾼들을 위한 오두막, 피크닉 공간, 배구 코트, 폐타이어 놀이터, 그리고 일광욕장까지 조성되어 있어 유기적이고 흥미로운 놀이 경관을 만들어낸다. '낚시꾼의 해변'이라는 이름은 이곳을 이용하던 낚시꾼들에게서 영감을 받은 것이다. 낚시꾼들은 계획 초기에는 회의적이었

The Centre for Environmental and Landscape Interpretation is built in a modular system using recycled maritime containers.

지만, 공원이 완성되어가는 과정에서 과거 그들을 불러들였던 장소성이 여전히 남아있음에 공감했다. 지역 낚시꾼들이 이 공원을 꾸준히 이용하면서 자발적인 관리에 참여하도록 유도했으며, 지역 커뮤니티와의 연계를 통해 지속가능성을 가진 공간을 만들고자 했다.

해양 컨테이너를 재활용하여 만든 '환경경관연구센터'는 전시회 등의 일시적인 이벤트를 열 수 있는 공간으로 지반으로부터 띄워져 있어 대상지를 따라 흐르는 광대한 생태계를 보다 편하게 바라볼 수 있다. 콘크리트 슬래브로 만들어진 대상지 내부의 보행로는 전체 공간을 면으로 구획하며 동시에 나눠진 공간을 연결한다. 식물은 자생종을 클러스터 형태로 식재했으며, 구획에 쓰인 나무 막대기는 모래가 유실되지 않도록 잡아주면서 사람들이 식재 구역을 훼손하지 않도록 유도한다.

번역 양다빈

Bird Observatory built from old pallets

ENOTA

Velenje City Center Promenada

Design ENOTA(Dean Lah, Milan Tomac, Tjaž Bauer, Andrej Oblak, Polona Ruparčič, Nuša Završnik Šilec, Alja Černe, Nebojša Vertovšek)
Structural Engineering Elea iC
Mechanical Services Nom biro
Electrical Planning Elsing
Client Velenje Municipality
Location Velenje, Slovenia
Area 17,020m²
Budget €2,700,000
Completion 2014
Photographs Miran Kambič, Roman Bor

South entrance of reactivation area

Velenje is a special city. As new post-war town, its design was based on the modernist ideal of the "garden city" and as such, it is unique in the Slovene space. The Velenje Promenada is an important city space and a vital city thoroughfare. It is one of the key axes of the city centre, which is why it can't be considered separately from the other city space within the context of the planned renovation. The intervention into the space must naturally be designed locally, in a way that allows an execution in stages, as provisioned in the project's budget. Still, it makes sense to outline the vision of the revitalization of the entire city centre. In this way, the spatial intervention is given a wider framework, which will ensure an informed sitting into the present and future city space.

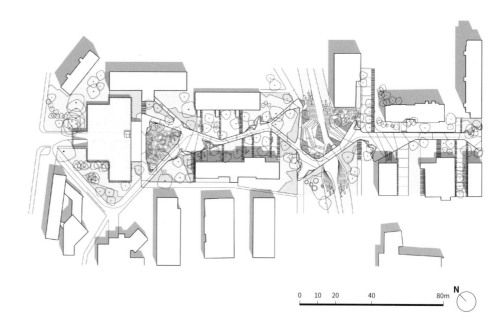

The green area of the park is to be extended across both banks of the Paka,
all the way from the school complex buildings on one side and
the Cultural Center and the former coal-mine administration building on the other.

The Park

At present, the area of the park is on the northern bank of the Paka, enclosed by the river on
one side and by the delivery road to the school complex on the other. The visitors to the park
don't have a real contact with the river, as the torrential canal of the Paka is liberally overgrown
with vegetation. The southern bank of the river serves as a public car park. In accordance with
the projection of removing the traffic and parking surfaces from the inner city centre, the green
area of the park is to be extended across both banks of the Paka, all the way from the school
complex buildings on one side and the Cultural Center and the former coal-mine administration
building on the other. Paka's relatively deep riverbed now divides the area into half, but by
modifying the riverfronts and creating a stepped approach towards the water level, it becomes
the area's central element. In several places and on several levels, both riverfronts are connected
into a unified whole. Footbridges extend into the network of paths on either bank, terminating
at the existing passages between the buildings. So as to achieve better integration into the
unified design of the park, the existing delivery and emergency routes are slightly modified.
In combination with some of the rigid surfaces, they retain their function to a large extent yet
visually, they are subsumed into the network of footpaths.

Newly created mounding area in Tito's Square

Commercial Street

Cankarjeva Road is already the heart and soul of the city. Its retail character must be retained and enhanced by means of additional programmes. Covering a part of the street from the library to the promenade would allow an intensive use of the space even in adverse weather. Such city space would allow for all kinds of open-air market events such as a flea market, an art fair, etc., which would no longer be weather-dependent.

Commercial Street terminates in Tito's Square. The square is part of the initial design of the town; it has its place in the townspeople's consciousness and has an indisputable cultural and historical role. But today, this is a large(possibly too large) and insufficiently articulated surface, and this may well be the reason why the plaza only fills up on rare occasions. In order to invigorate this part of the town, additional programmes are desperately needed to attract visitors.

After the closing down of the former marketplace, the most suitable location for a new one is being sought. One of the possibilities is for it to be placed beneath the surface of Tito's Square. Clearly, the intervention needs to be carried out so as not to modify the plaza's character, but only to accentuate its contour and add a bit level articulation to its surface to make it stand out from the other city surfaces and, crucially, attract a greater number of visitors and passers-by.

This will ensure that even when no special events are taking place, the plaza is still populated. The accommodation of the retail programme poses the opportunity to build a parking garage below the ground level, which would eliminate the majority of public car parks in the vicinity and put an end to the parking behind the Cultural Center and the municipality building. This would free up additional city surfaces, which can then be given over to public programme.

Promenada

The existing promenade was created by closing the erstwhile traffic road almost thirty years ago. Even though it was re-paved, a sufficiently thorough transformation never took place and the promenade has retained the character of a road, remaining too wide and rather dull due to the lack of content. It has been a kind of hybrid space between the road and the surface intended for pedestrians-chiefly a straight path quickly leading the users of the secondary-school complex and the community health centre to the inner centre without providing any animation for those out for a walk.

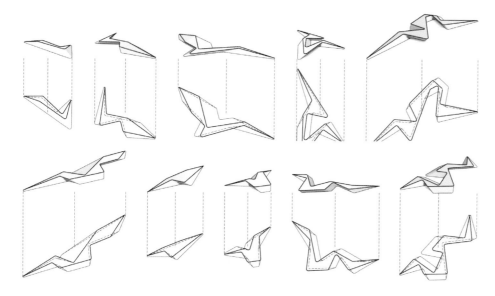

Bench diagram by type

A space organization system was introduced to reduce the huge spatial of the whole park area including Tito's Square.

340

Depending on the location, shape and size of the surrounding buildings, the curved walkways are organically connected to each other to form a larger open space.

Through renovation, the wide straight connection with a clearly delineated beginning and termination underwent a transformation into a kind of sequence of micro-ambients, of locally widened surfaces connected by a slightly twisting narrower path. These instances of widening(in effect squares) feature attractive concrete urban elements(benches) whose careful arrangement slows down the users and provides focus, framing the space for the additional programme content to take place. As the path locally twists along the surrounding buildings, it gives rise to larger contained open spaces, allowing future expansion of the content from the buildings outwards, or the accommodation of other additional content as required over time. In the initial phase, all these newly-formed public spaces are simply and cost-effectively laid out as sand or grass surfaces, with sand surfaces in particular representing a successful middle ground between grass and paved city spaces and allowing a wide range of use with only modest investment

With the transformation, the Promenada is turning into a main event axis of the city, its centre being placed into the new amphitheater along the river. The river Paka is a torrential river, which means that its watercourse swells up significantly a few times a year, but remains relatively shallow at all other times. As a consequence, the riverbed is very deep and until now, the river, which is an attractive element of any city, flowed out of sight somewhere down below. The wide bridge also meant that anyone walking across it had a hard time seeing the river at all. By narrowing the bridge and placing it off the former axis, the space for the construction of an amphitheater, which slowly slopes down towards the river surface, is recovered. The attractive amphitheater by the river, with the new bridge serving as its backdrop, becomes the centre of the activity in the city, and the river may once again claim an important spot in the townspeople's consciousness.

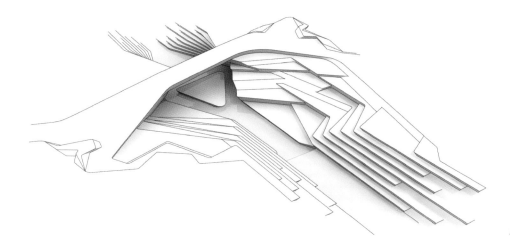

Amphitheater and bridge zone plan

슬로베니아 북동쪽에 자리하고 있는 벨레녜는 1950년대에 등장한 '전원 도시'라는 이상적 근대 도시 개념에 기초하여 계획된 도시로 현재 슬로베니아 도시 중 다섯 번째로 큰 규모다. '벨레녜 시티 센터 프롬나드(이하 벨레녜 프롬나드)'는 벨레녜 도심의 중심축을 구성하는 공공 공간으로서 도시 중심 가로에 새로운 활력을 불어 넣고 있다. 벨레녜 프롬나드는 도심 재활성화 사업의 첫 번째 단계로 추진된 프로젝트로 도시에 부족한 프로그램을 공급하고 벨레녜가 처음 조성될 당시 도입되었던 '공원 속의 마을'이라는 도시 조성 개념을 되살리는 것이 목표다. 기존 벨레녜 프롬나드는 파카 강과 중심 가로 주변으로 도로나 주차장 등 차량 관련 부지가 과도하게 많다는 문제를 개선할 필요가 있었다. 따라서 보행자 중심의 가로 환경을 구성하기 위해 '공원', '상가 거리', '프롬나드'라는 세 가지 공간 조성 개념을 적용했다.

공원

파카 강의 북쪽 둑에 조성된 공원 구역은 한쪽 면은 강으로 그리고 다른 한쪽 면은 학교 단지를 향해 놓인 운송용 도로로 둘러싸여 있다. 이 구역은 강의 급류 구간으로서 안전을 고려하여 강으로의 접근을 제한하기 위해 식재 위주의 계획을 했다. 강의 남쪽 구역은 공영 주차장으로 이용된다. 도심에서 차량 도로와 주차 공간을 제한한다는 계획 방침에 따라 공원 녹지는 파카 강의 양쪽 둑과 스쿨 존, 나아가 문화 센터와 전 탄광 시설관리소까지 전체적으로 확장되었다.

상가 거리

상가 거리는 공원 구역에서부터 벨레녜 시 조성 당시 계획된 티토 광장까지 이어진다. 과거 이 광장은 국가 기념일이나 공휴일에도 문화 행사나 관련 프로그램이 거의 일어나지 않는 공간이었다. 따라서 도시 내 광장의 활성화를 위한 매력적인 프로그램의 도입과 새로운 상가 운영을 위해 가장 적절한 공간 배치 방식이 필요했다. 가장 큰 문제는 티토 광장이 필요 이상으로 거대했고, 이로 인해 광장에 인접한 공간들 간의 연계를 통한 시너지 효과를 기대할 수 없다는 점이다. 이러한 문제를 해결하기 위해 티토 광장 면 아래 공간을 상업 공간으로 이용하고 티토 광장을 새롭게 조직하는 방안이 제시되었다.

이와 같은 공간적 개입은 광장의 기존 특성이나 성격을 완전히 뒤바꾸려는 것이 아닌, 공간의 레벨이나 구배의 차이에서 오는 공간감을 극대화하려는 전략적 선택이다. 결국 새로운 모습의 티토 광장은 특별한 이벤트가 없는 날이더라도 항상 사람들이 붐비는 장소가 될 것이다. 더욱 많은 방문객과 소매 상점 등의 서비스 관련 프로그램을 유치함에 따라 기존 지상 주차 공간—광장 부근 공영 주차장, 문화 센터 후면 주차장, 관공서 빌딩 후면 주차장 등—의 상당 부분을 없앴고, 그로 인해 발생할 주차 공간 부족 문제를 해소하기 위해 광장 지하에 새로운 주차장을 만들었다.

With the transformation, the Promenada is turning into a main event axis of the city, its centre being placed into the new amphitheater along the river.

©Miran Kambič

©Miran Kambič

The amphitheater was built by layering the
platform in line with the shape of the river and
the change of the surface of the river.

프롬나드

기존 벨레녜 프롬나드는 약 30년 전 차량 도로가 폐
쇄된 곳에 조성되었다. 프롬나드를 따라 보행 도로가
새로 만들어지기는 했지만 이용이 많지 않았다. 기존
차량 도로의 특징이 남아 있어 사람이 이용하기에는
폭이 너무 넓었고, 가로 관련 프로그램을 적용하기도
어려웠기 때문이다. 새로운 프롬나드는 길과 대지의
경계에 놓인 일종의 보행 친화적 하이브리드 공간으
로서 도심 내부로의 이동을 용이하게 한다.

벨레녜 프롬나드의 중심 공간은 강변에 새로 조성된
원형 극장이다. 파카 강에 흐르는 급류는 그 속도가
상당하다. 또한 평소 얕게 유지되는 수위가 급류에
따라 상당한 수준으로 높아지는 일도 적지 않다. 이
러한 급류의 영향력이 수십여 년간 지속되면서 강바
닥의 침식 작용이 누적되었고 지금과 같이 높은 레벨
차이와 굽이친 형태의 강이 형성되었다. 원형 극장의
모습은 이러한 강의 모습을 그대로 받아들이는 형태
를 취한다. 기존 다리의 폭을 줄이면서 위치를 변경
하고, 강의 수면 변화 양상에 맞춰 선큰된 플랫폼을
겹겹이 구성하는 방식으로 원형 극장이 조성되었다.

기존 프롬나드에 유기적으로 연결되지 못한 몇몇 소
로가 도로 보수 과정에서 일부 확장된 대지와 연결되
면서 독특한 분위기의 이동 시퀀스 상의 변화가 일어
나게 되었다. 이러한 과정에서 선형으로 확장된 도로
곳곳에는 독특한 형상의 벤치가 놓이게 되었다. 이
콘크리트 재질의 벤치는 보행 방향을 유도하고, 보행
자 또는 자전거 이용자의 속도에 영향을 주어 사고를
미연에 방지한다. 나아가 도시 곳곳에서 일어나는 다
양한 프로그램에 주목할 수 있는 기회도 제공한다.

주변 건물의 위치와 형태 또는 크기에 따라 휘어진 보행로는 인접 공간과 유기적으로 연계되며 더욱 큰 오픈스페이스를 형성하게 된다. 이는 건물 외부 공간에서 벌어지는 콘텐츠의 변화와 확장을 유도하며, 시간이 지남에 따라 사람들의 필요를 충족시킬 수 있는 가로 공간으로 기능할 것이다. 티토 광장, 길, 파카 강변 등 기존의 경관이 지닌 가능성을 파악하고 지형지물에 맞춘 디자인을 통해 벨레녜 프롬나드는 전혀 새로운 모습으로 거듭났으며, 도시민들의 의식 속에 다시 한번 중요한 장소로 자리매김하게 되었다. **번역** 손은신

The new Tito Square is used as an event space for children at night.

©Roman Bor

©Miran Kambič

346

Veleneje Promenada became once again an important place in the consciousness of the citizens.

laK WORKS 1

landscape architecture Korea

2014

landscape architecture korea 환경과조경
309
2014. 01.

309인에게
조경의 리얼리티를
묻다
환경과조경
새로운 30년의 시작

landscape architecture korea 환경과조경
310
2014. 02.

landscape architecture korea 환경과조경
311
2014. 03.

landscape architecture korea 환경과조경
312
2014. 04.

landscape architecture korea 환경과조경
313
2014. 05.

landscape architecture korea 환경과조경
314
2014. 06.

landscape architecture korea 환경과조경
315
2014. 07.

landscape architecture korea 환경과조경
316
2014. 08.

landscape architecture korea 환경과조경
317
2014. 09.

landscape architecture korea 환경과조경
318
2014. 10.

landscape architecture korea 환경과조경
319
2014. 11.

landscape architecture korea 환경과조경
320
2014. 12.

2015

landscape architecture korea 환경과조경
321
2015. 01.

독길: 경제학의 오피을 이미
한 읽리미에스 풀럽익 이크
크레도로리 사티 워크
MBC 상암 신사옥

landscape architecture korea 환경과조경
322
2015. 02.

TOPOTEK 1

landscape architecture korea 환경과조경
323
2015. 03.

landscape architecture korea 환경과조경
324
2015. 04.

landscape architecture korea 환경과조경
325
2015. 05.

landscape architecture korea 환경과조경
326
2015. 06.

landscape architecture korea 327 2015. 07.

landscape architecture korea 328 2015. 08.

landscape architecture korea 329 2015. 09.

landscape architecture korea 330 2015. 10.

landscape architecture korea 331 2015. 11.

landscape architecture korea 332

2016

landscape architecture korea 333 2016. 01.

landscape architecture korea 334 2016. 02.

landscape architecture korea 335 2016. 03.

landscape architecture korea 336 2016. 04.

landscape architecture korea 337 2016. 05.

landscape architecture korea 338 2016. 06.

landscape architecture korea 339 2016. 07.

landscape architecture korea 340 2016. 08.

landscape architecture korea 341 2016. 09.

landscape architecture korea 342 2016. 10.

landscape architecture korea 343 2016. 11.

landscape architecture korea 344 2016. 12.

lak WORKS